No More Butts

KICKING THE TOBACCO HABIT

Tobacco: The Deadly Drug

Born to Smoke: Nicotine and Genetics

Burning Money: The Cost of Smoking

But All My Friends Smoke:
Cigarettes and Peer Pressure

But Smoking Makes Me Happy: The Link Between
Nicotine and Depression

Cash Crop to Cash Cow:
The History of Tobacco and Smoking in America

False Images, Deadly Promises:
Smoking and the Media

No More Butts: Kicking the Tobacco Habit

Putting Out the Fire: Smoking and the Law

Smokeless Tobacco: Not a Safe Alternative

Teenagers and Tobacco:
Nicotine and the Adolescent Brain

Thousands of Deadly Chemicals:
Smoking and Health

No More Butts

Kicking the Tobacco Habit

by
Joan Esherick

No More Butts: Kicking the Tobacco Habit

MASON CREST PUBLISHERS INC.
370 Reed Road
Broomall, Pennsylvania 19008
(866)MCP-BOOK (toll free)
www.masoncrest.com

First Printing

9 8 7 6 5 4 3 2 1

ISBN 978-1-4222-0236-4
ISBN 978-1-4222-0230-2 (series)
        Library of Congress Cataloging-in-Publication Data
Esherick, Joan
No more butts : kicking the tobacco habit / Joan Esherick.
    p. cm. — (Tobacco: the deadly drug)
 Includes bibliographical references and index.
 ISBN 978-1-4222-0236-4   ISBN 978-1-4222-1330-8
 1. Smoking cessation—Juvenile literature. I. Title.
 HV5740.E74 2009
 616.86'506—dc22
                        2008013215

Design by MK Bassett-Harvey.
Produced by Harding House Publishing Service, Inc.
www.hardinghousepages.com
Cover design by Peter Culotta.
Printed in The United States of America.

Contents

Introduction *6*

1 Why Quit? Motivations to Stop Smoking *11*

2 Who's in Charge? *29*

3 Kicking the Habit the Medical Way *43*

4 Kicking the Habit the Behavioral Way *55*

5 Other Smoking-Cessation Strategies *71*

6 Ready for Anything: What to Expect When You Quit *83*

7 Smoke-Free for Life: Tips for Tossing Tobacco for Good *95*

Further Reading *103*

For More Information *104*

Bibliography *106*

Index *109*

Picture Credits *111*

Author/Consultant Biographies *112*

Introduction

Tobacco has been around for centuries. In fact, it played a major role in the early history of the United States. Tobacco use has fallen into and out of popularity, sometimes based on gender roles or class, or more recently, because of its effects on health. The books in the Mason Crest series TOBACCO: THE DEADLY DRUG, provide readers with a look at many aspects of tobacco use. Most important, the series takes a serious look at why smoking is such a hard habit to break, even with all of the available information about its harmful effects.

The primary ingredient in tobacco products that keeps people coming back for another cigarette is nicotine. Nicotine is a naturally occurring chemical in the tobacco plant. As plants evolved over millions of years, they developed the ability to produce chemical defenses against being eaten by animals. Nicotine is the tobacco plant's chemical defense weapon. Just as too much nicotine can make a person feel dizzy and nauseated, so the same thing happens to animals that might otherwise eat unlimited quantities of the tobacco plant.

Nicotine, in small doses, produces mildly pleasurable (rewarding) experiences, leading many people to dose themselves repeatedly throughout the day. People carefully dose themselves with nicotine to maximize the rewarding experience. These periodic hits of tobacco also help people avoid unpleasant (toxic) effects, such as dizziness, nausea, trembling, and sweating, which can occur when someone takes in an excessive amount of nicotine. These unpleasant effects are sometimes seen when a person smokes for the first time.

Although nicotine is the rewarding component of cigarettes, it is not the cause of many diseases that trouble smokers, such as lung cancer, heart attacks, and strokes. Many of the thousands of other chemicals in the cigarette are responsible for the increased risk for these diseases among smokers. In some cases, medical research has identified cancer-causing chemicals in the burning cigarette. More research is needed, because our understanding of exactly how cigarette smoking causes many forms of cancer, lung diseases (emphysema, bronchitis), heart attacks, and strokes is limited, as is our knowledge on the effects of secondhand smoke.

The problem with smoking also involves addiction. But what is addiction? Addiction refers to a pattern of behavior, lasting months to years, in which a person engages in the intense, daily use of a pleasure-producing (rewarding) activity, such as smoking. This type of use has medically and personally negative effects for the person. As an example of negative medical consequences, consider that heavy smoking (nicotine addiction) leads to heart attacks and lung cancer. As an example of negative personal consequences, consider that heavy smoking may cause a loss of friendship, because the friend can't tolerate the smoke and/or the odor.

Nicotine addiction includes tolerance and withdrawal. New smokers typically start with fewer than five cigarettes per day. Gradually, as the body becomes adapted to the presence of nicotine, greater amounts are required to obtain the same rewarding effects, and the person eventually smokes fifteen to twenty or more cigarettes per day. This is tolerance, meaning that more drug is needed to achieve the same rewarding effects. The brain becomes "wired" differently after long-term exposure to nicotine, allowing the brain to tolerate levels of nicotine that would otherwise be toxic and cause nausea, vomiting, dizziness and anxiety.

When a heavy smoker abruptly stops smoking, irritability, headache, sleeplessness, anxiety, and difficulty concentrating all develop within half a day and trouble the smoker for one to two weeks. These withdrawal effects are generally the opposite of those produced by the drug. They are another external sign that the brain has become wired differently because of long-term exposure to nicotine. The withdrawal effects described above are accompanied by craving. For the nicotine addict, craving is a state of mind in which having a cigarette seems the most important thing in life at the moment. For the nicotine addict, craving is a powerful urge to smoke.

Nicotine addiction, then, can be understood as heavy, daily use over months to years (with tolerance and withdrawal), despite negative consequences. Now that we have definitions of *nicotine* and *addiction*, why read the books in this series? The answer is simple: tobacco is available everywhere to persons of all ages. The books in the series TOBACCO: THE DEADLY DRUG are about understanding the beginnings, natural history, and consequences of nicotine addiction. If a teenager smokes at least one cigarette daily for a month, that person has an 80 percent chance of becoming a lifetime, nicotine-addicted, daily smoker, with all the negative consequences.

But the series is not limited to those topics. What are the characteristic beginnings of nicotine addiction? Nicotine addiction typically begins between the ages of twelve and twenty, when most young people decide to try a first cigarette. Because cigarettes are available everywhere in our society, with little restriction on purchase, nearly everyone is faced with the decision to take a puff from that first cigarette. Whether this first puff leads to a lifetime of nicotine addiction depends on several factors. Perhaps the most important factor is DNA (genetics), as twin studies tell us that most of the risk for nicotine addiction is genetic, but there is a large role for nongenetic factors (environment), such as the smoking habits of friends. Research is needed to identify the specific genetic and environmental factors that shape a person's decision to continue to smoke after that first cigarette. Books in the series also address how peer pressure and biology affect one's likelihood of smoking and possibly becoming addicted.

It is difficult to underestimate the power of nicotine addiction. It causes smokers to continue to smoke despite life-threatening events. When heavy smokers have a heart attack, a life-threatening event often directly related to smoking, they spend a week or more in the hospital where they cannot smoke. So they are discharged after enforced abstinence. Even though they realize that smoking contributed strongly to the heart attack, half of them return to their former smoking habits within three weeks of leaving the hospital. This decision to return to smoking increases the risk of a second heart attack. Nicotine addiction can influence powerfully the choices we make, often prompting us to make choices that put us at risk.

TOBACCO: THE DEADLY DRUG doesn't stop with the whys and the hows of smoking and addiction. The series includes books that provide readers with tools they can use to not take that first cigarette, how they can stand up to negative peer pressure, and know when they are being unfairly influenced by the media. And if they do become smokers, books in the series provide information about how they can stop.

If nicotine addiction can be a powerful negative effect, then giving people information that might help them decide to avoid—or stop—smoking makes sense. That is what TOBACCO: THE DEADLY DRUG is all about.

— *Wade Berrettini MD, PhD*

CHAPTER

Glossary

aneurysms: fluid-filled sacs in the wall of an artery that can weaken the wall.

D.A.R.E. programs: drug abuse resistance education programs, which help kids gain the skills they need to avoid abusing drugs and alcohol as well as engaging in other destructive behaviors.

mucus: the clear, slimy, lubricating substance, consisting mostly of mucins and water, that coats and protects mucous membranes.

nicotine: a poisonous alkaloid that is the chief active ingredient in tobacco and is also used in insecticides.

persevere: to persist in something, usually over a long period and despite problems and difficulties.

respiratory system: the system of organs in the body responsible for the intake of oxygen and the expiration of carbon dioxide.

stroke: a sudden blockage or rupture of a blood vessel in the brain, resulting in a loss of consciousness, partial loss of movement, or loss of speech; sometimes leads to sudden death.

Why Quit? Motivations to Stop Smoking

For Alicia, it was seeing her aunt struggle through the final stages of lung cancer.

For Jerome, it was his constant cough and increasing shortness of breath.

For Becca, it was the lingering odor she couldn't get out of her hair, clothes, and car.

For Frankie, it was a girlfriend's comment about his foul breath and yellow teeth.

And for Toni, it was the expense. She just couldn't afford to buy a pack a day anymore.

These young adults each made the decision to quit smoking, but each one had different motivations to give up cigarettes.

Though they had different reasons for quitting, they did have something in common besides their desire to stop smoking: None had any idea what to expect. They did know, however, that their nicotine habits were interfering with their lives.

Take Toni, for example. At $5 a pack per day, cigarettes cost this hardworking high school senior an average of $150 a month. That's equivalent to approximately ten CDs, seven DVDs, four or five manicures, about four tanks of gasoline for her car, thirteen movie tickets, an MP3 player, or 130 iTunes downloads each month! Toni decided she'd much rather have things like these to show for her wages than thirty packages' worth of smoked cigarette butts.

Or Frankie. He didn't realize, when he tried his first cigarette, that years later the small white cylinders he lit up each day would yellow his teeth, stain his fingers,

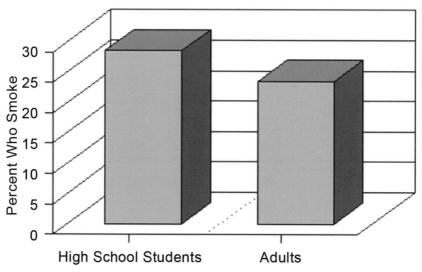

According to the Centers for Disease Control and Prevention, a higher percentage of teenagers smoke than adults, perhaps because teenagers think the dangers of smoking will never affect them.

dry out his skin, and make him smell like an ashtray. But they were a big turnoff to his girlfriend, who threatened to break up with him if he didn't quit. She didn't want to be seen with a guy with a gross smile and bad breath. And she certainly didn't want to kiss him!

Like Toni, Frankie, and the others, today's well-educated teens and young adults know about the hazards of smoking. They've seen photos of diseased lungs in their *D.A.R.E. programs* and health classes. They've heard people with cancer tell stories of how they wish they'd quit smoking sooner or never started to begin with. They're familiar with the risks.

Yet many young people end up smoking despite these and other antismoking programs. No one is sure why. Perhaps it's because many teenagers, the age group at greatest risk of starting to smoke, think the health dangers associated with smoking will never affect them. Or maybe it's because teens live in the moment, love to rebel, don't think much about tomorrow, and rarely consider the long-term effects of tar and *nicotine* on their bodies. Many begin smoking for the same reason they do other things—good and not so good. They do it because their friends do; it's peer pressure, the desire to impress people important to them.

Regardless of why teenagers begin, once they start and have been smoking for a while, they realize an important truth: *Smoking costs.* And for many, like the teens whose stories began this chapter, those costs are just too high to keep paying.

The Cost

In 1964, the surgeon general of the United States, the nation's highest-ranking public health officer, issued the first surgeon general's report on the health effects of smoking. Since then, Americans have known that tobacco products can harm, disable, or kill them. Whether they use cigarettes, cigars, pipes, or smokeless forms of tobacco, most smokers know that tobacco and its related chemicals cause or contribute to several forms of cancer, as well as *aneurysms*, cataracts, gum disease, pneumonia, cardiovascular disease, and respiratory diseases.

What surprises many people is how great other tobacco-use expenses have become. At the 2007 state-average price of $4.50 per pack (according to the U.S. Department of Agriculture), it costs over $1,600 a year to support a pack-a-day cigarette habit. That works out to more than $130 a month. Over an average smoking life span of sixty years (assuming the smoker starts at age fifteen and dies at seventy-five), that's a lifetime sum of $96,000! Forty years after the first surgeon general's report on smoking, the 2004 surgeon general's report cited these other increasing costs:

- In 2002, the medical cost of treating smoking-related cancers in the United States was more than $170 billion.
- Between 1964 and 2004, government officials attributed more than 12 million deaths to smoking-related illnesses.
- Between 1995 and 1999, the economic costs of smok-

ing in the United States (medical treatment, prescriptions, lost time from work, reduced work efficiency, etc.) totaled $157.7 billion each year, or $500 million dollars a day.

- Each adult who smokes reduces his or her life expectancy (how long he or she can expect to live) by an average of thirteen to fourteen years.
- The tobacco industry spends $13.4 billion per year—or over $36 million per day—on advertising and marketing, trying to convince people to use their products.
- Exposure to secondhand smoke (the smoke exhaled by smokers and inhaled by those who

Smoking-attributable expenditure (SAE) per maternal smoker, in 1996 dollars, by insurance status and area—United States

Area	Receiving Medicaid or uninsured		Private or other insurance	
	SAE per maternal smoker ($)	Prevalence (%)	SAE per maternal smoker ($)	Prevalence (%)
Alabama	750	16.4	670	8.0
Alaska	543	27.2	542	12.1
Arizona	649	11.6	585	5.7
Arkansas	753	23.4	664	11.7
California	674	15.5	437	8.9
Colorado	627	17.3	576	7.2
Connecticut	810	16.3	728	6.0
Delaware	863	19.0	733	9.1
District of Columbia	1,355	7.0	1,202	1.8
Florida	782	15.3	701	7.0
Georgia	799	13.4	715	5.9
Hawaii	523	12.8	507	4.6
Idaho	591	20.4	556	7.6
Illinois	844	18.2	700	7.8
Indiana	696	37.7	560	18.6
Iowa	700	29.0	643	11.4
Kansas	708	21.0	646	8.4
Kentucky	720	32.7	664	14.5
Louisiana	815	13.0	710	6.5
Maine	710	33.2	672	11.9
Maryland	882	16.0	739	5.8
Massachusetts	767	22.6	709	8.0
Michigan	775	26.7	677	11.0
Minnesota	714	21.4	650	7.8
Mississippi	813	14.9	695	9.0
Missouri	740	29.6	655	12.4
Montana	579	29.5	557	10.6
Nebraska	697	26.0	640	11.2
Nevada	678	17.9	595	9.2
New Hampshire	714	31.6	667	11.1
New Jersey	945	18.8	748	7.7
New Mexico	635	13.0	583	6.7
New York	842	20.4	582	8.1
North Carolina	804	20.7	703	9.2
North Dakota	643	32.0	624	13.0
Ohio	761	29.8	668	12.3
Oklahoma	717	23.5	666	9.8
Oregon	616	24.9	575	10.0
Pennsylvania	835	28.4	725	11.5
Rhode Island	769	27.2	685	10.6
South Carolina	806	18.1	710	8.9
South Dakota	564	28.2	566	12.6
Tennessee	778	23.0	683	10.6
Texas	755	9.6	692	4.4
Utah	587	16.0	550	4.8
Vermont	716	31.7	680	10.7
Virginia	830	16.6	719	6.4
Washington	610	23.2	577	9.2
West Virginia	710	34.1	676	14.2
Wisconsin	743	28.2	649	11.3
Wyoming	590	30.7	561	13.8
Total	245,284,878	19.3	120,851,759	8.8
Average	753		626	

Smoking is not just an expensive habit for individuals; society pays a high price in covering smoking-related costs through both government and private insurance programs. *Source: Morbidity and Mortality Weekly Report, October 8, 2004.*

aren't smoking the tobacco product) caused nearly $5 billion in health-related costs for non-smokers.

Sidebar: Smoking Hurts
Smoking hurts your . . .

• appearance
• health
• relationships
• physical fitness
• self-esteem
• emotional well-being

Add to these statistics the 700 to 900 people who die each year in fires started by unattended cigarettes, the more than 200,000 fires started by smoking-related materials, and the thousands of children whose lung functions become compromised because their parents smoke tobacco, and it's easy to see that using tobacco products does, indeed, cost a great deal.

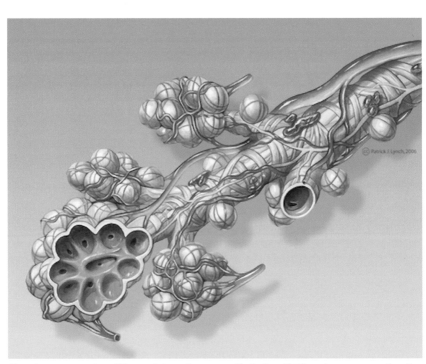

Your lungs contain millions of tiny air sacs called alveoli. The air sacs transfer the oxygen you breath into your blood, where it is transported throughout your body.

Chapter 1 • Why Quit? Motivations to Stop Smoking

17

If lost money, lost lives, and reduced life spans aren't enough to make someone want to quit, tobacco use impacts everyday health more than most people realize.

The Health Risk

Tobacco use almost always leads to health problems. The biggest known risk, of course, is cancer. Before cancer strikes, however, smoking can cause other, more subtle health changes.

"I used to be able to run a mile in under six minutes," states then-eighteen-year-old Kevin in an interview for the book *Heads Up: Real News about Drugs and Your Body*. "Now I'm lucky to make it in eight. And I'm wheezing all the way." At the time of the interview, Kevin had already reduced his cigarette use from two packs (forty cigarettes) to ten cigarettes a day. Despite the decrease, he still experienced symptoms that his smoking was affecting his health. As the star pitcher on his high school baseball team and one of the best golfers on the golf team, this young athlete could see how smoking was hurting his performance on the baseball diamond and the golf course. He wanted to quit.

Twenty-one-year-old Jenna wants to quit, too. In an interview with the American Council on Science and Health, she describes how smoking affects her in more graphic detail:

I get tired really quick. I used to be able to run the mile every Wednesday at

The Ultimate Price
Smoking kills more people than alcohol, AIDS, motor-vehicle accidents, illegal drugs, murders, and suicides *combined*. And that figure doesn't include deaths related to smokeless tobacco. (Source: Campaign for Tobacco-Free Kids, April 2007)

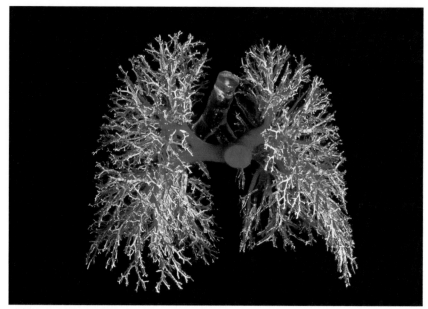

Tobacco smoke kills the alveoli in your lungs. They can't grow back, so every time you smoke you are destroying part of your lungs forever.

school in less than 10 minutes; now I would be lucky to make it through a full lap without having to stop and sit down in 10 minutes. Even when I am carrying groceries into the house, I have to stop and rest after about two armfuls. I can't even make it up a flight of stairs without having a problem.

[As far as energy goes] I have next to none. I wake up at 7 A.M. and go to class, take a nap at about noon, and go to bed at about 7 P.M. That is on a day when I don't really do much except walking and driving my car. I'm 21, I should be able to pull the all-nighters that my friends and I used to do all the time, but I can't.

I used to wake up in the middle of the night coughing so bad that I would have to use my inhaler. The

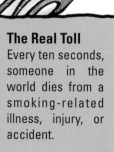

The Real Toll
Every ten seconds, someone in the world dies from a smoking-related illness, injury, or accident.

coughing used to get bad when I would try to do any kind of activity. I was even coughing sometimes when I would take a drag.

I was constantly hocking a lugie. It was always so thick in my throat. I would try to drink water or soda to make it go away; it never worked. I still

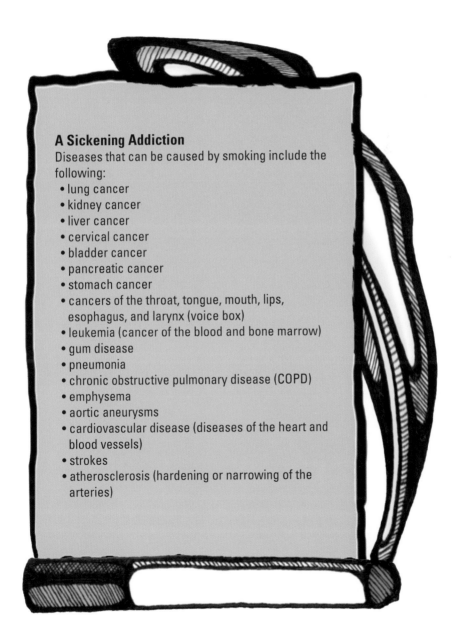

A Sickening Addiction
Diseases that can be caused by smoking include the following:
- lung cancer
- kidney cancer
- liver cancer
- cervical cancer
- bladder cancer
- pancreatic cancer
- stomach cancer
- cancers of the throat, tongue, mouth, lips, esophagus, and larynx (voice box)
- leukemia (cancer of the blood and bone marrow)
- gum disease
- pneumonia
- chronic obstructive pulmonary disease (COPD)
- emphysema
- aortic aneurysms
- cardiovascular disease (diseases of the heart and blood vessels)
- strokes
- atherosclerosis (hardening or narrowing of the arteries)

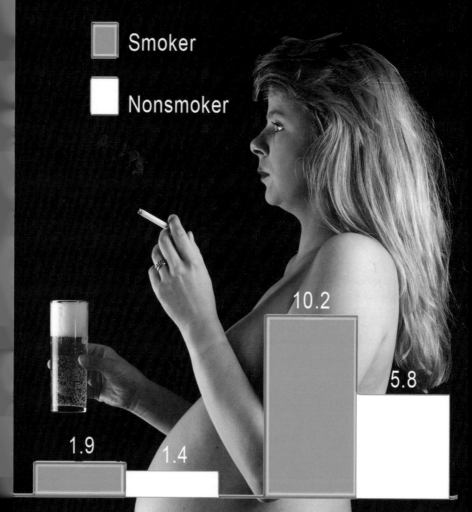

Percentage of Infants with Low Birth Weight, by Mother's Smoking Status, 1999

Smoker

Nonsmoker

10.2

5.8

1.9

1.4

Less than 1500 grams   1500 to 2499 grams

Source: Birth Certificates, CDC, NCHS, National Vital Statistics System.

Low birth weight babies born to women who smoked while pregnant are more likely to have health problems that require special care and longer hospital stays.

have *mucus* in my throat but have been getting better since I quit. Now I'm bringing up stuff from my lungs. It is not attractive to be spitting up green-colored stuff in front of guys; they actually get a really sick look on their face, like they are going to puke.

Jenna has tried to quit smoking twice before. Now on her third try, she has this to say about how her health is improving since she again gave up smoking: "Since

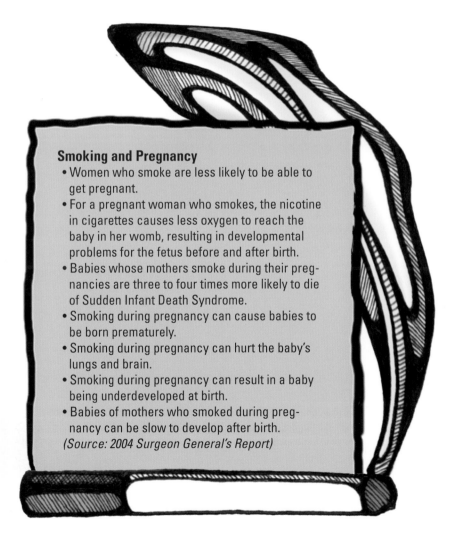

Smoking and Pregnancy
• Women who smoke are less likely to be able to get pregnant.
• For a pregnant woman who smokes, the nicotine in cigarettes causes less oxygen to reach the baby in her womb, resulting in developmental problems for the fetus before and after birth.
• Babies whose mothers smoke during their pregnancies are three to four times more likely to die of Sudden Infant Death Syndrome.
• Smoking during pregnancy can cause babies to be born prematurely.
• Smoking during pregnancy can hurt the baby's lungs and brain.
• Smoking during pregnancy can result in a baby being underdeveloped at birth.
• Babies of mothers who smoked during pregnancy can be slow to develop after birth.
(Source: 2004 Surgeon General's Report)

Carbon monoxide from tobacco smoke makes it harder for blood to transport oxygen to the body's cells, heart, and lungs. Less oxygen to the lungs means increased shortness of breath during sports and other physical activities.

I quit, I have been sleeping better and have enjoyed going for walks." She offers these additional words to anyone thinking about quitting or considering smoking for the first time:

> If you love doing any-thing that involves having to breathe, smoking will eventually make it impos-sible to continue. This hap-pens sooner [rather] than later, too. . . . Please don't smoke; it is just as bad as using drugs in many ways.
>
> I wish that I [had] never started.

Smoking Hurts Athletic Performance
Smokers are twice as likely to experience exercise-related injuries as nonsmokers.

(Source: American Journal of Preventative Medicine, 1996)

Jenna's and Kevin's experiences illustrate some of the more immediate health effects of smoking regularly: shortness of breath, decreased physical stamina, fatigue, mucus accumulation in the throat, an occasional cough (or a worsening cough when sick), and frequent colds and upper-respiratory infections. Other soon-to-appear side effects of smoking include the following:

- dry mouth
- frequent thirst
- nausea
- light-headedness
- stinging eyes
- pasty, coppery taste in your mouth
- increased heart rate

This list includes only the mild effects smokers experience soon after they begin lighting up regularly. After months, years, or decades of smoking, health issues become far more serious.

Various studies by the U.S. Centers for Disease Control and Prevention (CDC) and its Office on Smoking and Health have determined that regular use of nicotine products increases a person's risk of lung diseases, which is widely known, as well as fractures (bone breaks), sexual problems, reproductive problems, eye diseases, immune-system issues, and peptic ulcers. Researchers at these institutions have also determined that smokers who get sick take longer to get better. Smokers experience more complications after surgery, and often need to be hospitalized more often than nonsmokers.

It has been known for decades that smoking affects the body's *respiratory system*, but studies over the years have found that smoking's effects are not limited to that system alone. One of the major findings of the 2004 surgeon general's report was that smoking damages nearly every organ in the body. And because smoking harms the entire body, health issues can occur virtually anywhere. Consider these additional findings:

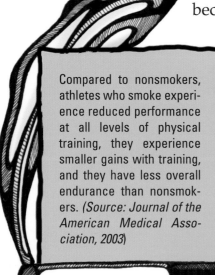

Compared to nonsmokers, athletes who smoke experience reduced performance at all levels of physical training, they experience smaller gains with training, and they have less overall endurance than nonsmokers. (*Source: Journal of the American Medical Association, 2003*)

• Smokers are ten times more likely than non-smokers to die from chronic obstructive pulmonary disease (COPD), the term for a group of diseases that affect the lungs, such as emphysema.

- Men who smoke are twenty-two times more likely to die from lung cancer as men who don't.
- Cigarette smoking nearly triples a person's likelihood of developing heart disease.
- Tobacco use doubles a person's risk of having a *stroke*.
- Smokers are ten times as likely to develop problems in the veins and arteries of their arms and legs as nonsmokers.
- Older women who smoke(d) experience far more hip fractures than women who never did.

Smoking-related health issues often become death rates. Consider these statistics from various 2006 CDC fact sheets:

- Tobacco use is the leading preventable cause of death in the United States.
- Every year in the United States, premature deaths from smoking rob more than 5 million years from the potential lifespans of those who have died.
- Cigarette smoking kills an estimated 259,500 men and 178,000 women in the United States each year.

Yes, smoking costs and smoking kills. But death rates, increased risk of health problems, and the financial burden aren't the only reasons smokers give for kicking the cigarette habit. Simply put, quitting can also help you feel better about yourself.

Social and Emotional Benefits

"I feel so much better about not exposing my friends and family to secondhand smoke."

"I just feel cleaner."

"I don't always feel guilty anymore."

"It seems like people who used to avoid me want to hang out with me now."

"Since I've been able to give up cigarettes, I feel like I can achieve whatever goals I set for myself."

"Ever since I quit smoking [my boyfriend] has been showering me with compliments and telling me how proud he is of me for quitting. My cousins like to hang out with me again now that I have quit. When I was smoking, they wouldn't even get in my truck because of the smell."

These quotes from real former smokers reflect some of the non–health-related motivations people have for giving up smoking: They don't want to feel guilty, they're tired of feeling like losers, they want to feel good about themselves. Sometimes this final reason, when weighed against the costs and health risks of smoking, is enough to push a smoker to make the decision to quit. Just as peer pressure might have led teens to smoke in the first place, it can also be a major force in helping them make the decision to quit.

Making the decision to quit smoking is just the first step, but it's a big one. But after deciding to quit, a person must persevere. Quitting is more difficult than it might seem.

CHAPTER

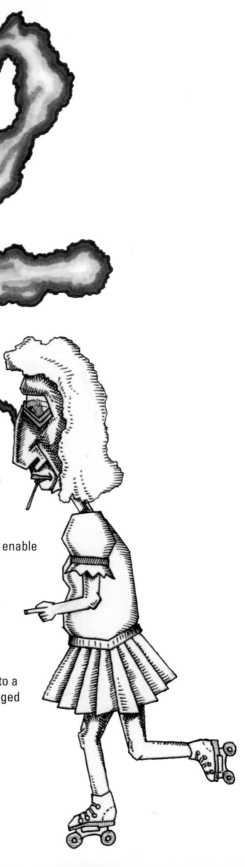

Glossary

hormone: a chemical secreted by an endocrine gland or some nerve cells that regulates the function of a specific tissue or organ.

neurotransmitters: chemical messengers that enable nerves to communicate with one another.

tangible: capable of being understood and evaluated.

tar: the residue from tobacco smoke.

tolerance: the reduction in the usual response to a drug as a result of use or exposure over a prolonged period.

Who's in Charge?

Nobody wakes up one day and thinks, "I'd like to die fourteen years sooner than I should or I'd love to have bleeding gums." No teenager goes out and pays a manicurist to split her fingernails and dye her fingertips yellow-gray. No twenty-something single uses ashtray-scented mouthwash before a big date. No athlete aspires to lose his ability to breathe, run well, taste food, or talk with a clear voice.

Yet, by choosing to use tobacco products, that's exactly what happens with each cigarette, cigar, or wad of chew they use. Sometimes they use tobacco and risk the health problems it can cause because they believe they are immune to such problems. Unfortunately, their beliefs are misplaced, and their

Teenagers might think twice about smoking if they considered its effects in other terms, such as inhaling carbon monoxide fumes directly from a car's exhaust pipe instead of from a cigarette.

understandings are limited, at best. Most smokers admit that they don't know what toxic substances are contained in the tobacco products they use. And most don't expect to become dependent on nicotine.

Hit Me!
An average smoker takes about ten puffs on a cigarette during the four or five minutes the cigarette stays lit. A person who smokes thirty cigarettes (about a pack and a half) per day gets about 300 hits of nicotine to his brain daily.

Think of it this way: Would you knowingly and willingly eat arsenic, a deadly toxin found in rat poison, that causes a slow, painful death? Would you drink the ammonia used to clean your kitchen floor? Would you sip formaldehyde from a lab specimen jar—the same jar biologists use to store dead frogs until they're used for dissecting? How about carbon monoxide: Would you plant yourself behind your car's exhaust pipe just to inhale its fumes? And then there's hydrogen cyanide: How does a trip to the gas chamber sound (yes, like the ones used during the Holocaust)? When you smoke, chew, or inhale, you expose your body to these poisons. These toxins hide in the tobacco products people use every day.

Most smokers know about the *tar* and nicotine in their tobacco products, but few realize the number of additional substances they contain. Astoundingly, every drag on a cigarette, every puff of a cigar, every draw on a pipe, or every wad of chewing tobacco wedged between the cheek and gum exposes the user to more than 4,000 identified chemical additives. Of these, more than sixty are known to cause cancer. A common nickname for a cigarette, "suicide stick," isn't far from the truth. Yet thousands more people become regular nicotine users each day. What gives?

Habit or Addiction?

It Starts Young

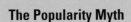

The Popularity Myth

A recent survey revealed these telling statistics: 67 percent of American teenagers said seeing someone smoke turned them off, 86 percent would rather date nonsmokers than smokers, and 65 percent strongly disliked being around smokers. Teenagers don't think smoking is cool.

The truth of the matter is that, generally speaking, adults don't start smoking; kids do. Ninety percent of tobacco users report getting hooked before they reached their nineteenth birthday. Sixty percent say they became addicted before they turned fourteen.

When asked why they started smoking, surveyed teenagers gave a variety of answers: "I was curious." "It was something to do." "My friends wanted me to try it." "I wanted to make my parents mad, and smoking seemed like the best idea at the time." "My big brother smoked and I wanted him to think I was in." "I thought I looked cool." "I wanted to look older." When they started, none of these teens expected to get hooked, and none expected to get hooked so fast. Virtually all thought they could control their tobacco use. Few knew anything about nicotine addiction.

Nicotine Causes a Physical Response

The U.S. surgeon general long ago concluded that nicotine is the drug in tobacco products that causes a person to become addicted. Nicotine is highly addictive. This addictive substance can enter the human body three ways: through the skin, the lungs, or the mucous membranes of the mouth, gums, and nose. It can also enter the body through the stomach.

Nicotine most commonly enters the body through the lungs. As smokers inhale, the nicotine in a cigarette immediately fills their lungs, where it is absorbed into the bloodstream. Researchers now know that within just eight seconds of being inhaled, absorbed nicotine travels to the brain. Within ten to fifteen seconds, as nicotine impacts the brain and body, smokers begin to feel

Prone to Panic
In a study reported on the American Cancer Society Web site (www.cancer.org), researchers reported that teenagers who smoke are more likely to experience panic attacks than teens who do not use tobacco. Smoking teens are also more likely to experience a range of other anxiety disorders as well.

Inhaling nicotine creates a feeling of well-being, but it is short-lived and can only be achieved again by smoking another cigarette.

nicotine's effects. The body reacts almost immediately.

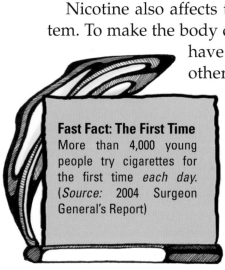

Bug Juice
After tobacco products, the next most common use for nicotine is as an insecticide.

When nicotine enters the brain, it first prompts a rapid release of the *hormone* adrenaline. Think for minute. When was the last time you had a really good scare? Perhaps a movie scene startled you, or you felt a rush after a near head-on collision with another car. The intense alertness, increased heart rate, spike in blood pressure, and rapid breathing you feel when you're startled comes from adrenaline; you've experienced an "adrenaline rush." Nicotine causes the body to react the same way it does during an adrenaline rush.

In addition to an increase in adrenaline level, nicotine causes the brain's neurons (nerve cells) to release more endorphins, the proteins the body uses as a natural painkiller and to create feelings of euphoria. The term *runner's high* refers to the impact endorphins have on the body and brain; in that case, as a result of exercise.

Nicotine also affects the brain's communication system. To make the body do what it needs to do, neurons have to "communicate" with each other. They do so by using chemical messengers called *neurotransmitters*. One of these chemical messengers is called dopamine, and it can cause feelings of pleasure and reward. Nicotine stimulates neurons in the brain to release higher-than-normal amounts of dopamine. When

Fast Fact: The First Time
More than 4,000 young people try cigarettes for the first time *each day*. (*Source:* 2004 Surgeon General's Report)

a smoker smokes, nicotine enters his lungs, bloodstream, and brain, creating an adrenaline rush, more endorphins, and a flood of dopamine, all resulting in feelings of pleasure.

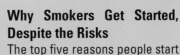

Why Smokers Get Started, Despite the Risks
The top five reasons people start smoking:
- popularity, to gain approval, or to fit in with the crowd
- to look cool or rebel
- to look older or more grown-up
- to lose weight
- curiosity

With an increase in adrenaline and dopamine, the smoker experiences an almost immediate rise in energy level, an increased ability to pay attention, greater alertness, and an improved ability to focus. This may be why some nicotine users say they can think more clearly or learn better after they've had a cigarette.

It's no wonder smokers become attracted to using tobacco products so fast. Nicotine causes nearly immediate, intense, positive feelings. In fact, researchers at the National Institute on Drug Abuse suggest that the effects of nicotine on the brain and body mimic those caused by other highly addictive drugs like cocaine and heroin. And it doesn't take many cigarettes to hook someone on these effects.

Never Enough

Only forty minutes after nicotine enters the body, more than half of its effects are gone. The intense alertness, clarity of thought, and feelings of euphoria, calm, and well-being have waned. The "wow" of pleasurable feelings has turned into "ho-hum." The "high" is starting to crash. After such intense pleasure, who wouldn't want more?

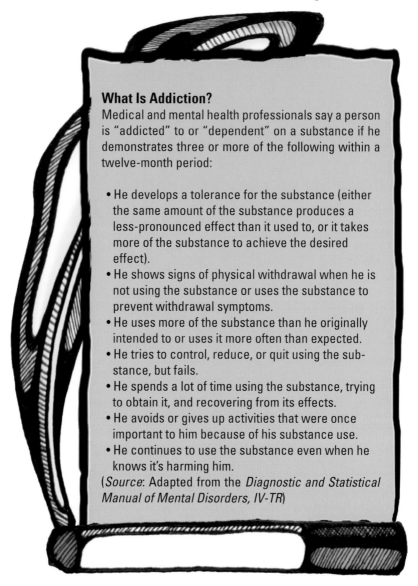

What Is Addiction?

Medical and mental health professionals say a person is "addicted" to or "dependent" on a substance if he demonstrates three or more of the following within a twelve-month period:

- He develops a tolerance for the substance (either the same amount of the substance produces a less-pronounced effect than it used to, or it takes more of the substance to achieve the desired effect).
- He shows signs of physical withdrawal when he is not using the substance or uses the substance to prevent withdrawal symptoms.
- He uses more of the substance than he originally intended to or uses it more often than expected.
- He tries to control, reduce, or quit using the substance, but fails.
- He spends a lot of time using the substance, trying to obtain it, and recovering from its effects.
- He avoids or gives up activities that were once important to him because of his substance use.
- He continues to use the substance even when he knows it's harming him.

(*Source*: Adapted from the *Diagnostic and Statistical Manual of Mental Disorders, IV-TR*)

It's only natural to want to experience pleasurable sensations over and over again. Because the smoker's body wants to experience nicotine-induced pleasure again, the smoker gets the urge to drag on another cigarette. But each time she inhales, she unknowingly changes her brain chemistry. Take dopamine, for example. When a smoker takes a puff of her cigarette, the nicotine tells the brain to release more of this pleasure-inducing neurotransmitter. The smoker's brain soon recognizes that it's released too much dopamine, and to guard against further excess the brain cuts back on its production of the neurotransmitter. Now, the smoker experiences a

Nicotine addiction results from a hard-to-break cycle of stimulation, tolerance, and dependency.

Fast Fact: Picking up the Habit
Every day, over 1,000 kids under 18 years old become new, regular, daily smokers. Of these, roughly one-third will die from smoking. (*Source*: Campaign for Tobacco-Free Kids, April 2007)

shortage of dopamine, leaving her feeling irritable and depressed. She "needs" more nicotine to stimulate more dopamine production so she can feel better—so she can feel the way she did before. With each cigarette, the cycle continues. As time goes on, the smoker develops a *tolerance* to nicotine; she needs more and more nicotine to produce the same effect less nicotine once produced. Her cravings become more intense. By then, she's fully addicted.

Tobacco users know well the physical dependency they develop on nicotine. But they'll tell you that dealing with physical dependency is easy compared to dealing with the mental and emotional ways they've come to rely on the drug.

The Psychological Response

What if someone told you he'd discovered an easy-to-swallow, immediate-acting "power pill" that could help you relax, concentrate, feel energetic, control your anger, maintain or lose weight, cope with stress, and handle pain? You'd probably buy it in a heartbeat; many people would. And after taking it for a while, you might begin to believe you've truly found the power.

Smoking, smokers insist, does much of what our imaginary power pill claims to do. And it's these benefits smokers are most reluctant to give up. When a recent poll asked smokers why they continued to smoke despite knowing the health risks, it wasn't fear of withdrawal symptoms from physical addiction that kept them from quitting; it was the reluctance to give up the psychological boost nicotine provided. Smoking, to the smoker, offers *tangible* benefits in the here and now, even if it robs him of his health in the long run. Though they may hate nicotine's side effects,

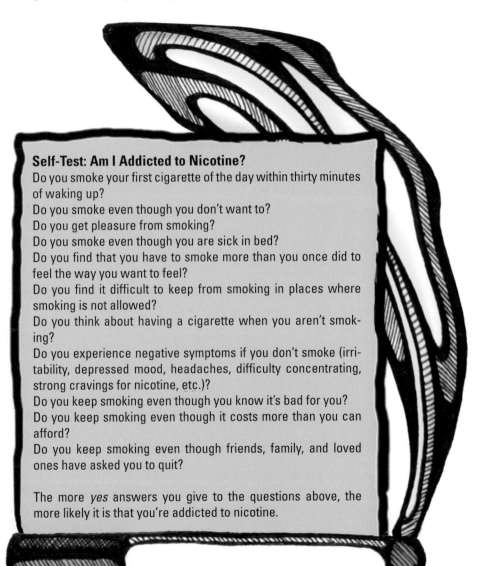

Self-Test: Am I Addicted to Nicotine?
Do you smoke your first cigarette of the day within thirty minutes of waking up?
Do you smoke even though you don't want to?
Do you get pleasure from smoking?
Do you smoke even though you are sick in bed?
Do you find that you have to smoke more than you once did to feel the way you want to feel?
Do you find it difficult to keep from smoking in places where smoking is not allowed?
Do you think about having a cigarette when you aren't smoking?
Do you experience negative symptoms if you don't smoke (irritability, depressed mood, headaches, difficulty concentrating, strong cravings for nicotine, etc.)?
Do you keep smoking even though you know it's bad for you?
Do you keep smoking even though it costs more than you can afford?
Do you keep smoking even though friends, family, and loved ones have asked you to quit?

The more *yes* answers you give to the questions above, the more likely it is that you're addicted to nicotine.

many smokers *like* the feeling they get from smoking. To the nicotine addict, smoking feels good. But feelings can trick us.

Not What They Seem

Many smokers claim that smoking makes them feel calm. Nicotine may reduce their bodies' physical reac-

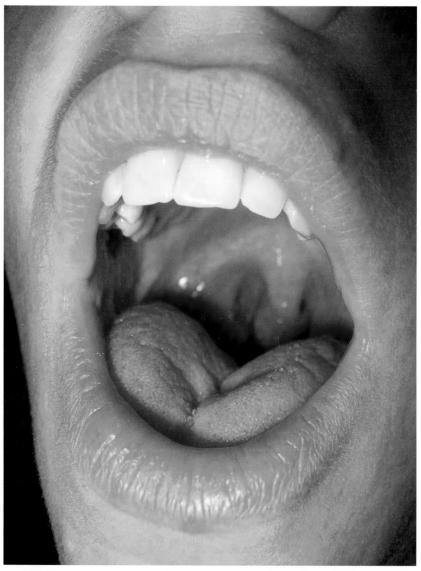

Smoking can cause depressions to develop on the surface of the tongue.

tions to not having nicotine (the shakes, jittery feelings, and agitation that can come with withdrawal), but it's the use of nicotine and then its stoppage that actually produced these symptoms to begin with. Smokers convince themselves that nicotine soothes them, when it is the very cause of their agitation.

Here's another example of how feelings trick smokers into believing something that's not exactly true. Some smokers insist that smoking helps them feel better about themselves. They're convinced that smoking makes them look better. But studies have shown that smoking does not improve appearance.

In 1985, Douglas Model, a British physician, came up with a term to describe what he consistently observed about smokers' facial skin, bone structure, lips, and eyes. Called "Smoker's Face," this condition commonly includes prune-like wrinkles radiating from the lips and eyes, a slightly gray skin color, hollow cheeks, and gaunt, bony facial features. People who smoke, Dr. Model concluded, have faces that look too old too soon.

Some smokers believe that smoking makes them look more sophisticated. After all, images of stars in all their bling holding a cigarette are fairly common. But that picture is incomplete. Those "sophisticated" stars are also subject to smoking's cosmetic downsides, including yellow teeth, tar stains on their teeth and fingers, watery eyes, ash burns, ashtray breath.

For many reasons, most smokers eventually decide to quit. The good news for them is that today's treatments for nicotine addiction usually do work. And quitting smoking yields almost immediate benefits for everyone who quits. How a person quits, however, varies with the individual.

CHAPTER 3

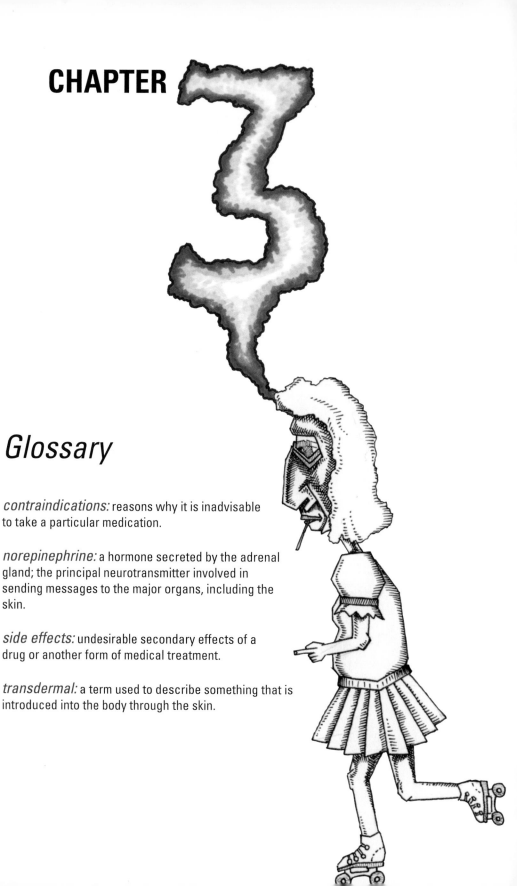

Glossary

contraindications: reasons why it is inadvisable to take a particular medication.

norepinephrine: a hormone secreted by the adrenal gland; the principal neurotransmitter involved in sending messages to the major organs, including the skin.

side effects: undesirable secondary effects of a drug or another form of medical treatment.

transdermal: a term used to describe something that is introduced into the body through the skin.

Kicking the Habit the Medical Way

Making the decision to stop using tobacco products is the first step—a huge step—toward living a nicotine-free life. But it's only the first decision. The next is *how* you'll quit. *What method or strategy will I use to help me give up nicotine for good?* Some strategies focus on helping the nicotine addict overcome his psychological or behavioral dependencies on tobacco. Others reject traditional science and medicine in favor of more "natural" methods. The most common ones address the physical aspects of nicotine addiction by using supplemental drug treatments to ease withdrawal symptoms.

While some tobacco users give up nicotine "cold turkey" on their own, most find they need help to succeed in quitting for good. We now turn to several methods former smokers have used to successfully kick their nicotine addictions.

Medical Strategies

An important thing to remember about all medically based strategies is that they use medicines—that is, drugs—to help a smoker quit smoking. Just as you have to be careful how you use medications your doctor prescribes or over-the-counter painkillers like ibuprofen or acetaminophen, you have to be careful when using these medicines to overcome nicotine addiction. They're drugs, and they should be used only as directed.

Nicotine Replacement Therapy

Nicotine replacement therapy (NRT) does exactly what its name implies: It replaces the nicotine your body receives from tobacco products with nicotine from safer sources. This eases the physical symptoms of nicotine withdrawal by allowing the body to have decreasing amounts of nicotine over longer periods of time. It's a weaning process, allowing those addicted to nicotine to ingest smaller and smaller doses until they no longer experience withdrawal symptoms.

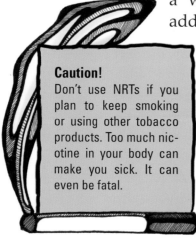

Caution!
Don't use NRTs if you plan to keep smoking or using other tobacco products. Too much nicotine in your body can make you sick. It can even be fatal.

The U.S. Food and Drug Administration (FDA) has approved five methods of nicotine replacement: patches, gum, nasal spray, oral inhalers, and throat lozenges. All have been approved for adult use only;

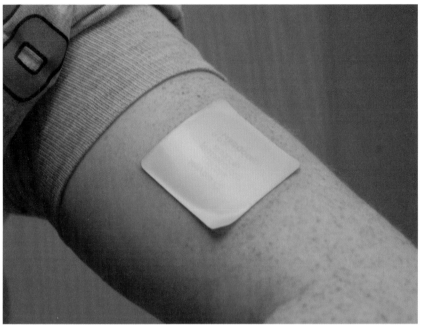

Nicotine patches work by weaning a person slowly off nicotine until their withdrawal symptoms diminish and eventually disappear.

teenagers are permitted to use these products only with the approval and supervision of a doctor.

Nicotine Patches

Also called *transdermal* nicotine systems, nicotine patches provide a measured dose of medication through a person's skin. Each patch looks like a half-dollar-sized disk of light cotton fabric with adhesive on the back. Adults can buy these patches at a drugstore without a doctor's prescription, but they should closely follow the instructions included in the product's packaging.

Patches come in several types and strengths. Some are designed for sixteen-hour use, while others can be used for twenty-four hours. Regardless of type or dose amount, all patches can cause unwanted *side effects*, even when used properly. The most common side effect is redness or itching of the skin where the patch is applied. More uncommon side effects include dizziness, headache, nausea, vomiting, muscle stiffness, body aches, racing heartbeat, and sleep disturbances.

Nicotine Gum

Nicotine gum is essentially chewing gum laced with nicotine. Because it allows nicotine to be absorbed through the mouth's mucous membranes, it usually works quickly. Like the nicotine patch, nicotine gum comes in various dose amounts and is available for sale

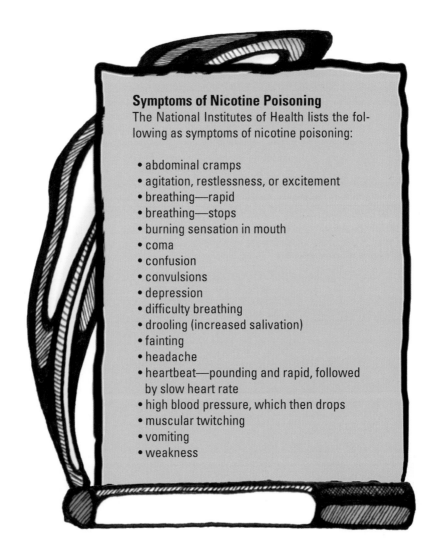

Symptoms of Nicotine Poisoning
The National Institutes of Health lists the following as symptoms of nicotine poisoning:

- abdominal cramps
- agitation, restlessness, or excitement
- breathing—rapid
- breathing—stops
- burning sensation in mouth
- coma
- confusion
- convulsions
- depression
- difficulty breathing
- drooling (increased salivation)
- fainting
- headache
- heartbeat—pounding and rapid, followed by slow heart rate
- high blood pressure, which then drops
- muscular twitching
- vomiting
- weakness

to adults without a prescription. Some former smokers say they prefer nicotine gum to other replacement strategies because it allows them to better control their nicotine doses. They can chew the gum as needed, especially during cravings, as long as they don't exceed the recommended maximum use.

This replacement strategy also has potential side effects: bad taste, mouth sores, jaw soreness, throat irritation, hiccups, nausea, and a racing heartbeat.

Nicotine Nasal Sprays

Since the nicotine in nasal sprays is absorbed through the mucous membranes of the nose, it rapidly enters the bloodstream and quickly produces desired effects.

Nicotine withdrawal can cause irritability, anxiety, and depression, which is part of the reason it is so hard to quit smoking.

This NRT, however, can be purchased only with a doctor's prescription and used only under her supervision. Doctors usually recommend that their patients use these nasal sprays for a limited amount of time.

Though easy to use, sprays often cause annoying side effects. But these typically last only two weeks, sometimes less. Some of the potential side effects users may experience are runny nose, watery eyes, sneezing, coughing, throat irritation, and nasal irritation. According to the *Physicians' Desk Reference*, people with certain medical conditions may not be able to use these nasal sprays. These contraindications include uncontrolled high blood pressure, allergies, and ulcers.

Nicotine Oral Inhalers

Oral inhalers deliver a puff of vapor containing nicotine to the mouth, not to the lungs as many presume. The

Nicotine gum is popular among former smokers because it allows them to better control their nicotine doses.

vapor is absorbed into the blood-stream via the mucous membranes lining the mouth. Like nicotine nasal sprays, a doctor's prescription is necessary to get nicotine inhalers. Oral inhalers are expensive, but some former smokers report that they prefer them because nicotine inhalers come as close to smoking a cigarette as one can get without actually smoking. They say inhaling the vapor felt good, almost like smoking. Nicotine inhalers also seem to cause fewer and less severe side effects. Some users reported minor coughing at first, mild throat irritation, and an occasional upset stomach.

> **The *Physicians' Desk Reference***
> The *Physicians' Desk Reference* is a published compilation of manufacturers' prescribing information for prescription drugs. It provides physicians with the full legally required information relevant to writing prescriptions. The information contained in the book is also provided on the package inserts that come with the medications.

Nicotine Throat Lozenges

Nicotine throat lozenges are the newest of the FDA-approved smoking-cessation methods. The lozenges are like hard candies, except they contain small doses of nicotine. The nicotine is released as the users suck on the lozenges. As with nicotine patches and gums, adults do not need a doctor's prescription for this smoking-cessation aid; they can buy these lozenges at their local pharmacy.

As with all other replacement strategies, lozenges can cause unexpected and troublesome side effects: difficulty sleeping, headaches, flatulence (intestinal gas), heartburn, coughing, hiccups, and dizziness.

All NRTs—lozenges, oral inhalers, nasal sprays, gums, and patches—come highly recommended as proven strategies for combating the physical component of nicotine addiction. But because NRTs contain nicotine, you should use them only after consulting with a physician, and only if you've already stopped using other nicotine products.

Medicines without Nicotine

Many doctors find that NRTs alone don't help a smoker overcome her addiction. They address only the physical aspects of nicotine withdrawal and not other aspects. For more complete support in overcoming addiction, NRTs should be used with other methods of quitting, including prescription drugs that don't contain nicotine.

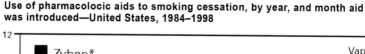

Use of pharmacolocic aids to smoking cessation, by year, and month aid was introduced—United States, 1984–1998

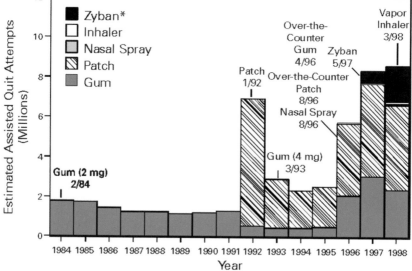

*Use of trade names and commercial sources is for identification only and does not constitute endorsement by CDC or the U.S. Department of Health and Human Services.

A variety of products are available to help smokers in their attempt to quit the habit.

Zyban® (Bupropion Hydrochloride)

One of the most widely prescribed drugs used to help people stop smoking is Zyban. Usually used to treat depression, Zyban targets certain neurotransmitters in the brain that can be affected by nicotine, including dopamine and *norepinephrine.*

Though it does not contain nicotine, Zyban does affect brain chemistry. Because it does, you can take it only with a doctor's prescription and under his supervision. It shouldn't be used by individuals taking certain other medications or who have particular health conditions. For example, individuals with a seizure disorder or who have been diagnosed with bulimia or anorexia nervosa should not take Zyban. The medication has not been tested in children under the age of eighteen.

Zyban is not without its own risk of side effects, the most serious of which is seizures. According to the *Physicians' Desk Reference,* one in a thousand individuals who take Zyban will experience a seizure. The medication is contraindicated for individuals who have a seizure disorder, such as epilepsy. More common side effects include dry mouth and sleep difficulties.

Zyban may not be the best choice for every person trying to kick a tobacco habit, but for some, especially when used with other strategies, it can greatly improve their odds of quitting for good.

Chantix® (Varenicline)

As another prescription medicine and the only other non–nicotine-containing prescription drug used to help smokers quit smoking, Chantix is only available with a doctor's prescription. Like Zyban, this drug affects the brain's neurotransmitters, especially dopamine, and produces similar physical effects to those of nicotine.

In recent studies done by Pfizer, the drug's manufacturer, the most common side effects people experienced

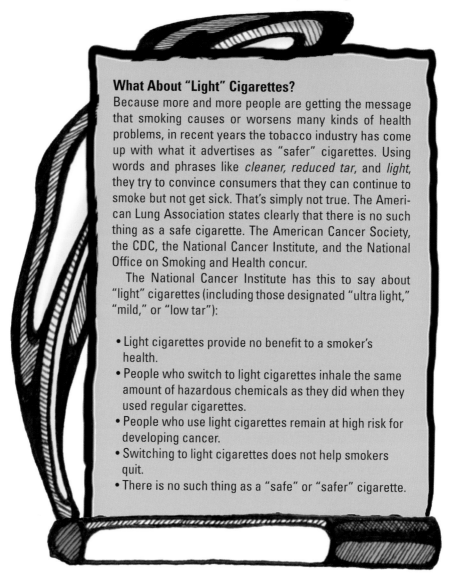

What About "Light" Cigarettes?

Because more and more people are getting the message that smoking causes or worsens many kinds of health problems, in recent years the tobacco industry has come up with what it advertises as "safer" cigarettes. Using words and phrases like *cleaner, reduced tar,* and *light,* they try to convince consumers that they can continue to smoke but not get sick. That's simply not true. The American Lung Association states clearly that there is no such thing as a safe cigarette. The American Cancer Society, the CDC, the National Cancer Institute, and the National Office on Smoking and Health concur.

The National Cancer Institute has this to say about "light" cigarettes (including those designated "ultra light," "mild," or "low tar"):

- Light cigarettes provide no benefit to a smoker's health.
- People who switch to light cigarettes inhale the same amount of hazardous chemicals as they did when they used regular cigarettes.
- People who use light cigarettes remain at high risk for developing cancer.
- Switching to light cigarettes does not help smokers quit.
- There is no such thing as a "safe" or "safer" cigarette.

when they took Chantix were nausea, changes in dreaming patterns, constipation, flatulence, burping, and vomiting.

Methods not Approved by the FDA

While prescription medications and NRTs make up the greatest percentage of medically based treatment methods, there are other methods on the market that claim to be effective in combating nicotine addiction. After all, nicotine addiction is big business. It provides tobacco companies with lots and lots of money. But, in recent years, battling nicotine addiction has become equally as big a moneymaking industry. Some companies advertise their products as the next "cure" for smoking, though they lack scientific evidence to back up their claims. That lack of scientific data doesn't stop them from promising instant relief from nicotine cravings. Like snake-oil hawkers of old, they make outrageous claims because they want your buck.

Some of these companies advertise their products in newspapers and magazines or on TV and radio programs. You may have read about or heard of their products: nicotine lollipops or tobacco lozenges or anti-craving lip balms. But beware. The FDA hasn't reviewed or approved these things, and it can be dangerous to use products that have not been tested and approved.

For many people, NRTs and prescription medications have proved to be effective tools in their quest to stop smoking. According to some reports, quit rates are approximately 25 percent for individuals using NRTs, 35 percent for those using Zyban, and 45 percent for those taking Chantix during short-term (twelve-week) clinical trials. For those who need extra help or for whom medical interventions are not appropriate, there are other ways to kick the smoking habit.

CHAPTER 4

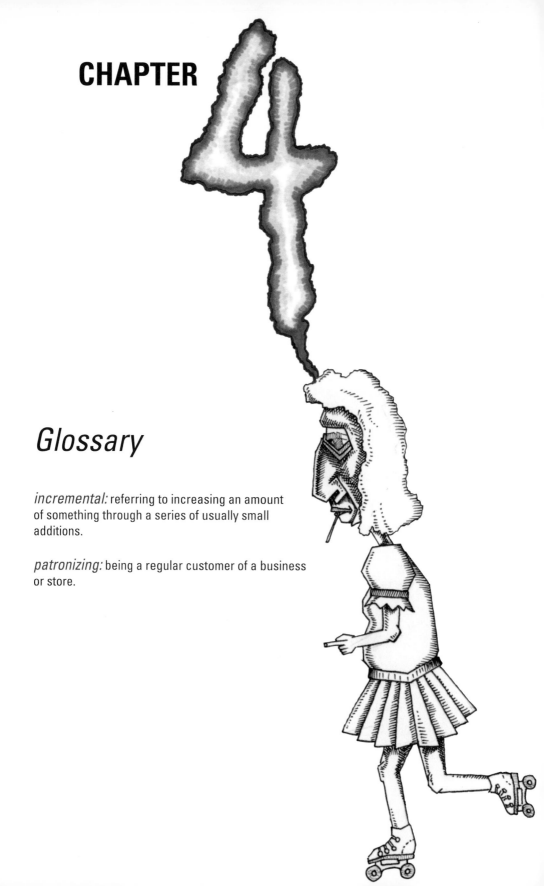

Glossary

incremental: referring to increasing an amount of something through a series of usually small additions.

patronizing: being a regular customer of a business or store.

Kicking the Habit the Behavioral Way

"Some of my friends and family are smokers. They know I'm trying to quit, but they still smoke around me. How can I resist smoking when I'm around them? What should I do?"

"It's weird. Every time we break for lunch at work, I get this incredible urge to smoke. I've been nicotine-free now for four months, and I think the urges have stopped pretty much everywhere else but there. I thought it would be easier by now. How come it's still so tempting?"

"One of the hardest places for me to resist smoking is in the car. My car still smells like smoke, but I don't think that's it. I think it's because I didn't drive anywhere without having a cigarette between my fingers and the window cracked. Driving just feels normal that way to me. Now it feels like there's something missing. How can I get over that feeling?"

"Whenever I sit down and watch *Grey's Anatomy*, it seems like all I can do is think about having a cigarette. I thought watching TV would distract me, but it seems to make my cravings even worse. What's that all about?"

These questions highlight a fact scientists have known for decades: circumstances, thoughts, memories, habits, and emotions can make smokers crave cigarettes every bit as much as brain chemistry can. And just as medicine can help reduce chemically and physically based cravings, certain behavior-modification strategies can help reduce psychologically based cravings.

Behavior Modification

To break a habit or addiction, our behavior must change. Take a look at the stories that opened this chapter. Each of these individuals had certain situations that reminded them about smoking—and that tempted them to restart smoking. For them, and for anyone else trying to stop smoking, they must change behavior patterns in order to be successful.

Behavior modification is a psychological treatment method. The goal of this form of therapy is to change an individual's undesirable behavior by rewarding new and desirable ones. The undesirable behaviors are made less attractive. In time, the individual undergoing behavior-modification therapy will replace the old habits with new behaviors.

It's important to remember that change isn't going to happen overnight. It's a process that requires several steps along the way.

Meditation and yoga are healthier alternatives to smoking, but they provide many similar calming effects.

Identify and Eliminate Triggers/Cues

Think of a handgun. What happens when you pull the trigger? A series of events occurs within the gun's firing chamber to propel the bullet out of the barrel. The trigger makes the gun shoot; that is, the trigger makes something happen.

Psychological triggers work in a similar fashion. In the case of tobacco use, psychological triggers work in tandem with physiological triggers that cause your body to crave nicotine. Examples of psychological triggers include songs, smells, places, activities, emotions, and habits or routines.

Think about when you're most likely to smoke. If you always smoke while you're driving, your car may be a psychological trigger. If you always chew smokeless tobacco when you're playing baseball, the baseball diamond or the sights, sounds, and smells associated with baseball might be psychological triggers. If you always puff on a cigar when you go fishing, the activity of fishing may be a psychological trigger. If smoking is part of your dessert routine, then eating dessert may be a psychological trigger.

Psychological triggers usually include those people,

Weight Gain: Not a Given

Don't replace one bad habit with another. We've all heard people express concern that they'll gain weight if they stop smoking. And some people do. But that's not a given. Make sure to have low-calorie, sugar-free snacks on hand for those times when the urge to have a cigarette hits—and they will. With healthy snacks on hand, you'll be able to avoid high-calorie, less healthy foods and drinks that can make you pile on the extra pounds. Better yet, get up and move when you have the urge to smoke.

places, or things with which you associate smoking, such as the following:

- hanging out under stadium bleachers
- the smoker's lounge at work
- a favorite smoking-allowed restaurant or bar
- smoking friends
- attending pro sports events
- your after-school or work routine

When someone trying to quit using tobacco encounters a trigger like one of these, it can evoke strong cravings. These cravings might not be so much for a hit of nicotine as for the act of smoking itself. Many people

Smokers who are trying to quit can avoid psychological triggers by making a habit of going to smoke-free places, which are becoming more and more common.

find the following helpful in handling their psychological triggers:

1. *Identify your triggers.* If you don't know what triggers your desire to smoke, you can't be prepared to combat it. To figure out what your triggers are, establish a quit date, the exact date that you're going to stop smoking or chewing tobacco. Before your quit date, keep track of when, where, and with whom you most often smoke. These may be your triggers.

2. *Avoid exposure to your triggers.* Try eating at restaurants that don't allow smoking. Make a habit of going to smoke-free public places, like the mall,

Changing your daily routine so that your activities don't revolve around smoking can increase your chance of success at quitting.

the public library, and the movie theater. Don't attend parties where you know people will be smoking.

3. *When you can't eliminate a trigger, plan for it.* Take a bunch of lollipops with you to your smoking friend's house. Ask your smoking friends and family not to smoke around you or leave tobacco products where you can see them. Instead of going to the smoking lounge during your lunch break, head to the smoke-free cafeteria. Instead of reaching for a cigarette after dinner, excuse your-self from the table and go brush your teeth.

Change It Up

Ice-hockey fans have probably heard a coach tell their players to "change it up" when one line needs refresh-ing or when they shift from offense to defense or defense to offense. Like hockey teams, you may need to "change it up" to overcome and defeat your psychological trig-gers.

To change it up, you simply change your routine. If you want to smoke right after you wake up, try getting up earlier and going for a walk instead of having a morn-ing cigarette. If driving your car triggers your cravings, try walking, biking, or taking the bus or train instead. If certain types of music make you want to smoke, switch radio stations or CDs, or create completely new playlists that won't be associated with your nicotine habit. Go to different restaurants or movie theaters than you're used to *patronizing*. Hang out with nonsmokers. Watch differ-ent TV shows. Sit at a different place at the dinner table. Change your scenery.

Changing it up should help you avoid some triggers without having to sacrifice the things you most enjoy. It

Just Wait It Out!
Scientists have shown that the urge to smoke lasts only three to five minutes. That's equivalent to

- the length of an average commercial break on TV
- the average time it take to reboot a PC
- the brewing time for a cup of tea
- the cooking time for a bag of microwave popcorn
- the average length of a song played on the radio
- less time than it takes to get dressed or put on makeup
- less time than the average shower
- less time than it takes to play one round of computer solitaire

allows you to live life without constantly encountering triggers. But changing it up won't completely eliminate stress.

Develop New Ways to Handle Stress

Like it or not, stress is a part of life. So what is stress? Briefly, it's the mental, emotional, or physical strain caused by things like overwork or anxiety. Everyone faces stress on a daily basis, but we each have our own way of handling the stress in our lives. And it has to be handled. Failure to handle stress effectively can cause its own set of severe health issues. So how do people deal with stress? Some people eat. Some shop. Others escape into television, pornography, or video games. Still others drink or get high. A few chew their fingernails or cut themselves. And some smoke. None of those methods are particularly healthy or beneficial.

But there are beneficial ways to address stress. One key to having a successful life (however you define it) is learning to manage stress in productive, healthy way, including the following:

- go for a walk
- exercise
- pray
- take your dog to the park
- meditate
- read
- keep a journal (written, video, or audio)
- drink a cup of soothing, herbal tea
- practice deep-breathing exercises
- do yoga
- start a hobby
- start a collection
- join a club, sports team, or online interest group
- volunteer at your local hospital, place of worship, recycling center, food bank, soup kitchen, or senior center

Managing stress should be *con*structive.

Behavioral Replacement Strategies

"What should I do with my hands?" That is a question asked by many people trying to stop smoking. To many smokers, the feeling of rolling a cigarette between their fingers and thumb is soothing, even if they aren't actually smoking. Former smokers report that this rolling action is easier to replace than to give up. So they roll pencils, drinking straws, cinnamon sticks, or lollipops between their fingers. They tap pens and paper clips. They take up hobbies to keep their hands busy: woodworking, painting, needlework, model building, gardening, and the like.

Replacement strategies help by equipping the smoker with tools to replace a formerly destructive behavior with a new, beneficial one. This is also the basis of behavior modification. Replacement strategies work, but they're far more effective when used together with other strategies, including psychological support.

Rally Support

Quitting smoking is *not* easy. When your world is full of psychological triggers, having solid psychological support can make the difference between quitting for a day and quitting for good.

Joining a support group can help with the feelings of loneliness experienced by many people who try to quit.

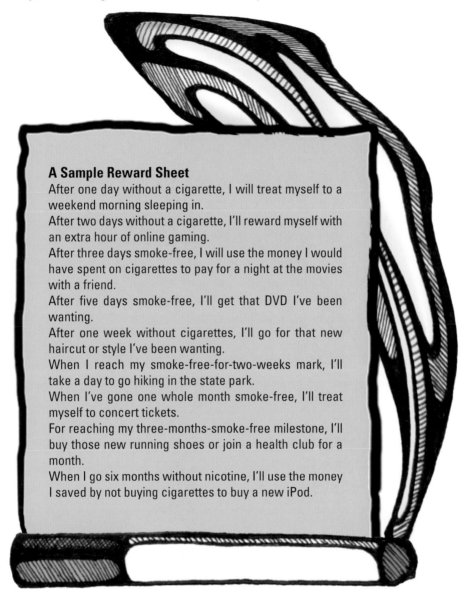

A Sample Reward Sheet
After one day without a cigarette, I will treat myself to a weekend morning sleeping in.
After two days without a cigarette, I'll reward myself with an extra hour of online gaming.
After three days smoke-free, I will use the money I would have spent on cigarettes to pay for a night at the movies with a friend.
After five days smoke-free, I'll get that DVD I've been wanting.
After one week without cigarettes, I'll go for that new haircut or style I've been wanting.
When I reach my smoke-free-for-two-weeks mark, I'll take a day to go hiking in the state park.
When I've gone one whole month smoke-free, I'll treat myself to concert tickets.
For reaching my three-months-smoke-free milestone, I'll buy those new running shoes or join a health club for a month.
When I go six months without nicotine, I'll use the money I saved by not buying cigarettes to buy a new iPod.

To recruit support for any quitting attempt, *tell* someone: friends, family, coworkers, your family physician, fellow students, supervisors, teachers, coaches, teammates. Tell whomever you plan to be around on your quit day and beyond. Be specific. Give them your quit date, and let them know how they can help. Or join a support group for those trying to give up the nicotine habit. Recruit another smoker to quit with you.

The more personal, emotional, and psychological support you have, the more likely it is you'll be successful in your attempt to rid yourself of nicotine forever. But what if there's no one to call when you're experiencing a craving and all your friends and family members are out of town?

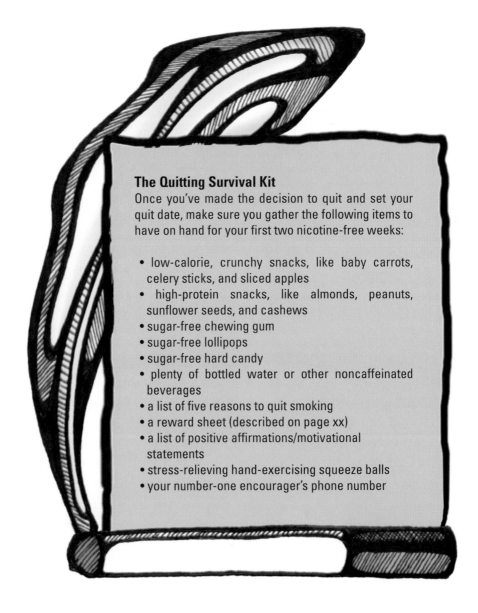

The Quitting Survival Kit
Once you've made the decision to quit and set your quit date, make sure you gather the following items to have on hand for your first two nicotine-free weeks:

- low-calorie, crunchy snacks, like baby carrots, celery sticks, and sliced apples
- high-protein snacks, like almonds, peanuts, sunflower seeds, and cashews
- sugar-free chewing gum
- sugar-free lollipops
- sugar-free hard candy
- plenty of bottled water or other noncaffeinated beverages
- a list of five reasons to quit smoking
- a reward sheet (described on page xx)
- a list of positive affirmations/motivational statements
- stress-relieving hand-exercising squeeze balls
- your number-one encourager's phone number

Talk to Yourself

According to former smokers, quitting smoking can create crushing feelings of loneliness. They report feeling as though no one in the entire world understands what they're going through. They believe no one else "gets it." Former smokers who believe they are alone in their struggle have fallen prey to another psychological aspect of smoking cessation: talking to yourself.

Yes, we all talk to ourselves. No, not aloud (okay, sometimes out loud), but most often we tell ourselves things in our minds. For the smoker trying to quit, it can be things like *I can't be happy without a cigarette*, or *My friends won't like me anymore if I quit*, or *I could calm down if I had just one cigarette*. What you tell yourself can make or break the quitting experience.

Try telling yourself the truth: *Yes, this craving is strong and feels awful, but it will be over in five minutes. I can wait it out. I don't need cigarettes to have fun. People who want the best for me are my real friends, and real friends don't want me to smoke. Smoking costs a lot of money. I can quit. It may be difficult, but I can do it.*

Reward Yourself

Goals are good things, but sometimes individuals set goals that can seem almost impossible to reach. Most people find it easier to reach their ultimate goal by setting smaller, more easily attainable goals that lead to the desired result. This strategy can also help with smoking-cessation plans. Of course, it helps if you plan for a little reward in there as well!

We all enjoy rewards. Rewards tend to motivate us and keep us working toward specific goals.

That's why companies offer bonuses, parents offer allowances for completed chores, teachers offer extra credit, and team fund-raisers offer prizes for the highest amounts raised. The idea of receiving a reward makes us want to work harder or stick to the plan. It's no differ-

Giving yourself regular rewards along the way will motivate you on your journey to living a life free of nicotine addiction.

ent with a plan to quit smoking, except that you reward yourself instead of waiting for others to reward you.

When you decide to quit, make a list of the rewards you plan for yourself or create a reward sheet. Include *incremental* rewards along the way. Let's say your first goal is to remain smoke-free for a day. When you've successfully completed that day, give yourself a small reward. The next goal could be to remain smoke-free for two days. Again, when that goal is realized, give yourself a reward, but this time one that's a little bigger. The biggest reward should come when you've reached your ultimate goal.

So what kind of rewards can you give yourself? Remember the young people whose stories began this book? Here's how they rewarded themselves:

- Alicia treated herself to a full manicure and pedicure.
- Jerome joined a health club.
- Becca bought new drapes and a few new outfits.
- Frankie saved up to get his teeth whitened.
- Toni put her money away for college fun.

These young adults learned the importance of rewarding themselves for each milestone they made in their nicotine-addiction recovery.

Looking forward to a reward can provide just enough motivation to make it through a craving. And it feels great when the reward actually comes! The greatest reward, of course, is the freedom you'll find when you're no longer enslaved by nicotine. A smoke-free life is a terrific reward, but be smart about which strategies you choose to help you reach your goal.

CHAPTER

Glossary

adjunct: something added to something else to increase its benefits.

efficacy: the ability to produce the desired result.

induces: produces, or brings about.

panacea: a supposed cure-all for all diseases or problems.

Other Smoking- Cessation Strategies

Although most people who want help to stop smoking choose medical or behavioral treatment methods, others look to alternative methods. Some seek quick and easy fixes, while others want to make sure they're aware of all available options.

Hypnosis

Many people have turned to hypnosis as a smoking-cessation treatment. A September 2007 Google search brought more that 690,000 hits to the search query "smoking cessation and hypnosis."

Is hypnosis effective in helping someone to stop smoking? According to a 2000 study reported in the *International Journal of Clinical and Experimental Hypnosis,* it might be. One of the study's coauthors, psychologist Joseph Green, reports that hypnosis does appear to have some effect on smoking-cessation efforts. But he warns, "Giving hypnosis the stamp of a well-established treatment for smoking cessation is premature." Though it's an effective treatment tool, it's not a *panacea.*

Not everyone responds to hypnosis, but some have found it helpful. Hypnosis *induces* an altered state of consciousness, which enables the mind to be more open to suggestions that help individuals gain control over behaviors—like smoking—that they want to change. Most studies on the *efficacy* of hypnosis have shown that it works best when used as an *adjunct* to behavior-modification therapies.

Acupuncture

Another alternative method used to stop smoking is acupuncture. Though it is relatively new in the West, acupuncture has been a part of traditional Chinese medicine for thousands of year. Acupuncturists insert fine-tipped needles at key points in the body to stimulate the flow of chi (what the Chinese call the body's life force or energy).

Proponents of acupuncture believe that the treatment can reduce withdrawal symptoms and cravings. Some people report that they have found relief through acupuncture, but little scientific research has been conducted on its effectiveness. As in the case of hypnosis, doctors generally recommend that acupuncture be used along with more scientifically validated smoking-cessation programs.

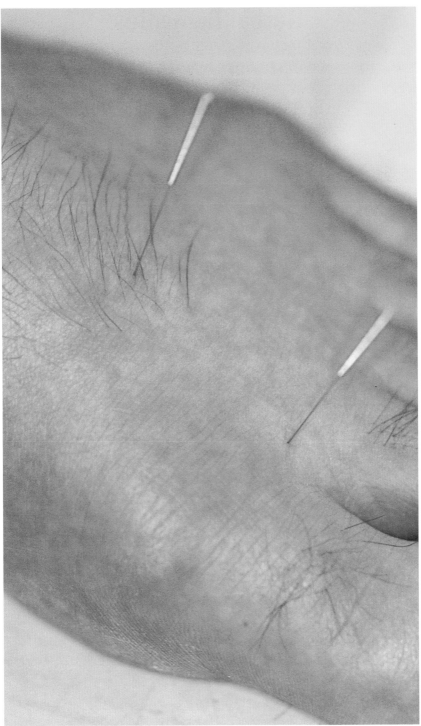

One theory about how acupuncture works suggests that it stimulates the release of endorphins, just as nicotine does.

Herbal Remedies

Some people believe that all herbs are safe. After all, they don't need FDA approval. That's the problem. For a drug to become available to the public in the United States, its manufacturer has to first prove that the drug actually works as intended and that it's safe to use as directed. After a drug has been proven safe and effective, the FDA approves the drug for sale or distribution through doctors, and the public can obtain it.

The FDA doesn't regulate herbs or herbal remedies because they aren't sold as medicines; they are marketed as dietary supplements. The manufacturers, therefore, don't have to follow the same laws as those who make drugs. They don't have to prove that their remedies work consistently, are effective, or are safe.

But just because herbs are not legally treated as drugs, that doesn't mean they do not have druglike effects on the body. They can sometimes interact with medications or other herbs in ways that can harm or even kill. For that reason alone, herbal remedies should only be used after consulting a health care professional.

Some companies tout the use of lobelia (also called Indian tobacco or pukeweed) as an aid to smoking cessation. There is no proof that it, or any other herb, can actually help a person stop smoking.

Programs That Work

By now, it might seem as though it's almost impossible to stop smoking without using some kind of medication. Though that might seem discouraging, there are smoking-cessation programs that really do work without requiring medication. These programs help thousands of Americans quit successfully every year. To be successful, you have to find a plan that will work for you. Not every plan works for everybody. What worked for your mom, your brother, or your best friend might not work for you. To help you get an idea of what's available, here are just a few of the most popular and most effective programs out there (all of them are free).

The Great American Smokeout (American Cancer Society)

Since 1977, the American Cancer Society has sponsored the Great American Smokeout on the third Thursday in November to encourage smokers to quit. This program establishes a quit date for those reluctant to set one for

Eating a healthy snack can be a substitute for the activity of smoking a cigarette.

themselves, and provides an opportunity to join others in quitting at the same time.

Loaded with helpful information, how-to-quit advice, stories of people who've successfully quit, practical tips, and personal support through hot lines and Internet counselors, the Great American Smokeout equips thousands of people each year with the tools to give up their nicotine habits once and for all.

Online Support

You can find a support group or chat room for almost anything on the Internet. For people who aren't comfortable in real-world groups or who live in places where there are no smoking-cessation support groups, the Internet can be a good place to find others undergoing similar experiences.

But beware. Not everything is as it seems on the Internet. Treat suggestions cautiously, keeping in mind that what worked for one person might not work for another. And remember: Though most people are on the Internet to help others and get help for themselves, there are an unscrupulous few whose motives are less than honorable. Avoid giving out personal information, such as your full name, address, or even your telephone number. And if someone wants to meet you, tell your parents. If they agree that the meeting is a good idea, get a group together and meet in a public place.

You Can Quit Smoking Now (U.S. Surgeon General)

This four-step program covers many of the same bases other programs cover; it just uses different names for each step. The U.S. government's official Web site for this program, www.smokefree.gov, outlines the program:

Step 1: Thinking About Quitting
- Why quit?
- What's in a cigarette?
- Reasons for quitting
  —Smoking's impact on others
- Why is quitting so hard?
  —Nicotine addiction test
  —Smoking triggers
  —Keep track of when and why you smoke

Step 2: Preparing to Quit
- Overview of the basic steps
- Set a quit date
- Tell others your plan to quit
- Anticipate and plan for challenges
  —Remove all tobacco
  —Talk to your doctor
  —Medicines that help with withdrawal
- Other support
  —Benefits of a quit-smoking program

Step 3: Quitting
- Steps to take on quit day
  —Use your support program
  —Keep busy
  —Stay away from what tempts you

- Managing cravings
  —Find new things to do
  —Remember instant rewards
  —Plan for the long-term rewards of being smoke-free
- Withdrawal symptoms
- What to do if you slip

Step 4: Staying Quit

- Sticking with it
  —Keep your guard up
  —Fight urges
  —Stay upbeat
  —Keep rewarding yourself
- Resources to help you if you slip up

The long-term rewards of not smoking are more than worth the effort required to quit.

Nicotine Anonymous®

Like the more familiar Alcoholics Anonymous, Nicotine Anonymous utilizes a twelve-step program to help people quit their tobacco addiction. The only requirement for membership is the desire to stop using nicotine products. Weekly meetings, being paired with a "sponsor" (a former smoker who will be there to help you stay on track), educational presentations and homework assignments, personal testimonies, and hanging around with group members make up much of the Nicotine Anonymous program. You should be able to find a Nicotine Anonymous program listed in your local telephone book. You can also use the "Find a Meeting" feature on the organization's Web site (www.nicotine-anonymous. org) to locate a group that meets near your home.

National Cancer Institute (NCI)

Like the surgeon general's You Can Quit Smoking Now program, the NCI offers a four-step plan:

1. Get ready.
2. Get medicine.
3. Get help.
4. Stay quit.

Individuals who successfully used the NCI plan say they liked the countdown hints it offers as they approached their quit dates (see "The NCI's Five-Day Countdown to Quit Date"). They felt the countdown gave them a checklist to follow while they prepared to quit. It also helped them get excited about and look forward to starting the plan. In addition, former smokers appreciated the NCI's toll-free hot line, a number staffed by smoking-cessation counselors they could call 24/7.

No Plan Is a Magic Cure

All these smoking-cessation programs are effective, but that doesn't mean they work for everyone. Sometimes people have to try a plan multiple times before it works for them. Keep the following things in mind when you're trying to choose what will work best for you:

1. Avoid smoking-cessation plans, programs, or substances claiming to have "secret" ingredients" or

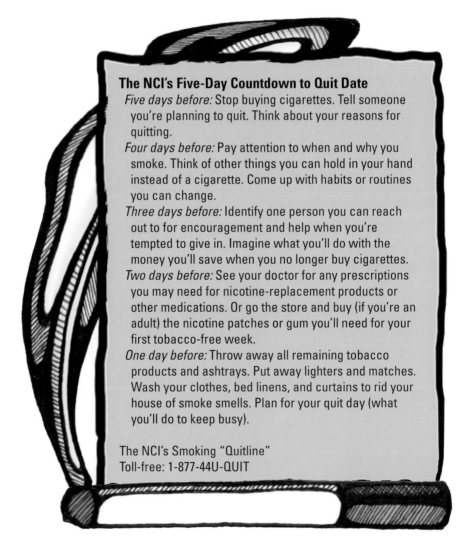

The NCI's Five-Day Countdown to Quit Date

Five days before: Stop buying cigarettes. Tell someone you're planning to quit. Think about your reasons for quitting.

Four days before: Pay attention to when and why you smoke. Think of other things you can hold in your hand instead of a cigarette. Come up with habits or routines you can change.

Three days before: Identify one person you can reach out to for encouragement and help when you're tempted to give in. Imagine what you'll do with the money you'll save when you no longer buy cigarettes.

Two days before: See your doctor for any prescriptions you may need for nicotine-replacement products or other medications. Or go the store and buy (if you're an adult) the nicotine patches or gum you'll need for your first tobacco-free week.

One day before: Throw away all remaining tobacco products and ashtrays. Put away lighters and matches. Wash your clothes, bed linens, and curtains to rid your house of smoke smells. Plan for your quit day (what you'll do to keep busy).

The NCI's Smoking "Quitline"
Toll-free: 1-877-44U-QUIT

that offer "instant success" or a "miracle solution" to the nicotine problem. Quitting smoking is difficult; there is no such thing as an easy cure.

2. Only a plan you can smoothly fit into your schedule will work. Choose one that will disrupt your normal daily life as little as possible.

3. Just because one smoking plan worked for your best friend doesn't mean it will work for you. Feel free to try a different plan. And if you relapse on one, try another. Don't feel locked into one approach.

4. Research demonstrates that a combination of strategies works best. For example, try doctor-supervised NRT with behavior-replacement strategies, along with a structured program where you can receive support. The more weapons there are in your giving-up-nicotine arsenal, the more likely it is you'll eventually defeat your addiction.

Once you've chosen your strategy, educate yourself on what to expect next. If you have an idea of what to expect once you quit, you'll be better prepared to face those challenges.

CHAPTER

Glossary

blindside: to take someone unawares suddenly, with detrimental results to that person.

relapse: to fall back into a former way of life.

Ready for Anything: What to Expect When You Quit

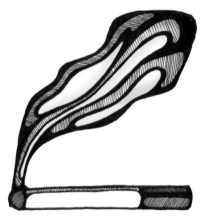

Setting the Stage

The first step to reaching any smoking-cessation goal is, of course, making the decision to stop smoking in the first place. The next step is to decide when.

Pick a day, any day. It might be a special day, like your birthday or New Year's Day or the day the American Cancer Society sets aside each year for the Great American Smokeout (it's always the third Thursday of November). Or it might be a week from now, or the first of next month, or the start of next week.

To set your quit date, first remind yourself about why you want quit. Write down your top five reasons on an index card, and tape it up where you're sure to see it each day. You should identify what means the most to you personally. To get you started, here are some reasons other smokers have come up with to motivate them to quit:

I want my clothes and hair to smell better.
I want to live a long, healthy life.
I want more energy.
I need more spending money.
I don't want to get cancer.
I want to have more control over my life.
I don't want to make others breathe my second-hand smoke.

Setting a quit date can increase your chance of success because it forces you to anticipate and deal with conflicting feelings that are sure to arise.

It might seem that setting a quit date is really no big deal, but carefully selecting the date can increase your likelihood of success. For example, people addicted to nicotine are often surprised by the conflicting emotions they feel about giving up smoking once they decide to do so. Yes, people who quit have firm reasons for quitting, but they also play tug-of-war with reasons they *don't* want to quit: *I really like smoking; I enjoy the camaraderie I feel with other smokers; I like how I feel when I smoke.* If you set a quit date, and you realize these that feelings might arise, you'll be better prepared and better able to deal with them, rather than allowing them to derail your efforts. That doesn't mean they won't still surface from time to time.

Be Ready to Argue with Yourself

Quitting smoking can make a person feel like the pushmi-pullyu (pronounced "push-me-pull-you") of Hugh Lofting's *The Story of Dr. Dolittle*. This fictional, gazelle-like beast had "no tail, but a head at each end, and sharp horns on each head." The smoker attempting to quit may find that he argues with himself, almost as if he'd developed two talking heads within his brain:

I want to quit because I know I'll be healthier, but I like how smoking makes me feel. Research says smoking will eventually kill me, but I sometimes feel like I can't live without it.

This internal debate can *blindside* smokers who want to quit and leave them

Social Smoking?
Almost everyone has heard of social drinking, but social smoking? Yes, there is such a thing. Some people only smoke when they are in social situations, such as at parties or at a bar or club. Though they may not smoke as much as someone who does so as part of everyday life, it still causes them harm.

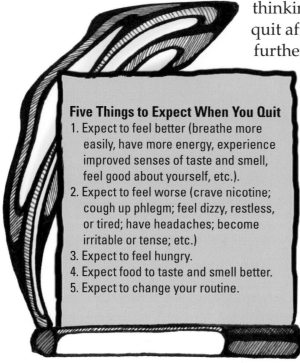

Five Things to Expect When You Quit

1. Expect to feel better (breathe more easily, have more energy, experience improved senses of taste and smell, feel good about yourself, etc.).
2. Expect to feel worse (crave nicotine; cough up phlegm; feel dizzy, restless, or tired; have headaches; become irritable or tense; etc.)
3. Expect to feel hungry.
4. Expect food to taste and smell better.
5. Expect to change your routine.

thinking they're not ready to quit after all. Nothing could be further from the truth. They are ready. This back-and-forth seesaw of thoughts and emotions is very common and perfectly normal. Expect it, recognize the conflicting thoughts for what they are—just honest feelings—and then remind yourself about why you want to quit. Knowing why you want to quit prepares you to do so. Then you're ready to begin.

Write Down Your Quit Date

Whatever day you choose as your quit date, mark it on your calendar. Tell a few people you trust when you plan to quit, and ask them to mark the date on their calendars, too. Sign up on the Internet or by phone to have someone from the American Cancer Society's Quitline contact you about your quitting plan. Then prepare for what you'll encounter as you begin your quitting experience.

Prepare Your Surroundings

If you don't have it, you can't use it. Sounds simple enough, but in actuality, something as simple as seeing an ashtray or smelling tobacco smoke on clothing can sabotage a smoking-cessation plan. So before your quit date:

- Don't buy any cigarettes, chewing tobacco, cigars, or other nicotine-containing products and throw out any you might still have. Be sure to ditch that "secret stash," too.
- Get rid of as many smoke smells as you can: Wash your hair and clothing; air out your curtains and drapes; open your windows; use fresheners on your throw rugs and carpets. Don't forget the car. Make sure to empty the ashtray and give the interior a good cleaning (including the inside of the windows).

When you have chosen a quit date, clear your surroundings of all smoking-related items, so you'll be ready to begin your new smoke-free life.

- Throw out *all* ashtrays, lighters, and matches.
- Anticipate the desire to have something in your mouth. Make sure to have mouth-stimulating substitutes on hand: sugar-free chewing gum, lollipops, hard candy, and healthy crunchy snacks like popcorn, almonds, whole-wheat pretzels, carrots, or celery sticks.
- Keep things available to occupy your hands: pens, pencils, rubber bands, Chinese hand-massage therapy balls, tension-release squeeze balls, or a lump of modeling clay. Take up knitting or crocheting—you can end up with a new scarf or hat while keeping your mind off cigarettes.
- Have on hand a supply of bottled water or other noncaffeinated beverages.
- Stock up on interesting reading material, hobby supplies, video games, computer games, or movies you'd like to watch so you'll always have something around to keep you busy.
- If you've chosen to use a nicotine replacement therapy, make sure you've stocked the necessary supplies (patches, gum, inhalers, etc.).

Prepare Your Friends and Family

Tell your smoking and nonsmoking friends alike about your plan to quit. Inform them of your quit date. Be prepared, however, for mixed reactions. Some will encourage you; others may want you to keep smoking. Remember: The choice is yours—not theirs—to make. It's your right to make the choice to be healthy.

Ask your smoking friends not to offer you cigarettes. Better yet, ask them not to smoke around you. Best ever, ask a smoking friend to quit with you. It will be better for both of you.

Ask your nonsmoking friends to keep you busy for the first few days or weeks following your quit date: Go to the movies, take walks together, hang out and watch DVDs, attend sports events, work out together. Go to places where smoking is prohibited. Recruit them to help you stay occupied so you're less likely to think about how much you miss nicotine.

Inform people with whom you live, go to school, work, or socialize that you may be crabby for the first few days after quitting. Ask them to be patient and to support you, then give them specific things they can do to help you get through your irritability: *Offer to go for a walk with me, take me to the gym, hand me a Tootsie Pop or*

A stress ball can give you something to do with your hands instead of holding a cigarette.

Popsicle, go to a movie with me, challenge me to a computer NASCAR race, or whatever you think will most help you get through this initial period.

Prepare Yourself for Temptation

Expect certain times, places, activities, and situations (especially those during which you used to use nicotine products) to make you want to smoke or chew even after you quit: playing baseball; taking a coffee break at work; driving your car; hanging out with smoking friends; drinking alcohol or coffee; having dessert; or going to parties, the bowling alley, or other places you associate with smoking. These triggers can make you think about lighting up. They can make you feel desperate to take a drag. They can make you miss smoking and cause you to *relapse*.

A support system made up of nonsmoking friends can help see you through the rough stretches.

Be encouraged, though. If you prepare for your triggers, you can avoid them or substitute new actions or activities for them.

Expectations

Expect Good and Bad Feelings

When you actually quit, two things will likely happen: You'll feel excited and proud about your decision to quit, and you'll feel nervous and intimidated by quitting. Again, like Dr. Dolittle's pushmi-pullyu, you'll experience conflicting emotions. Simply knowing that you will experience both positive and negative feelings prepares you to handle them more effectively. For example, you may feel great about the steps you're taking to make a healthier life choice, but you may hate how isolated from your still-smoking friends quitting makes you feel. You may be encouraged by how brave you feel tackling your addiction head-on, but fear the physical symptoms you know will come with nicotine withdrawal. You may seem revved up and motivated in your quest to give up nicotine, yet feel tired and depressed.

Expect the conflict. Then prepare yourself to handle it by reminding yourself over and over again why you really want to quit and recalling the benefits you'll experience when you do.

Expect to Crave Nicotine

We've seen how nicotine affects the body and the mind. And we've identified how the body, once used to getting regular doses of nicotine, will respond when it's deprived of its nicotine fix. When you quit smoking, know this: *You will crave nicotine.* But also know this: You *can* handle your cravings. Try these strategies:

- Tell yourself the craving will pass. It will. Just wait it out.
- Talk yourself out of your urge to smoke. Remind yourself of the gross side effects of smoking. Think about how awful phlegm feels in your throat and how unappealing it is to other people. Recall how your clothes used to reek. Remind yourself of how well you're doing and how much better you'll feel if you resist this urge instead of giving in to it.
- Call an encourager, someone who will support your attempt to resist your craving.
- Do something: Go for a walk, suck on a lollipop, play a video game, start a sudoku puzzle. Do whatever it takes to take your mind off your craving.

Don't Plan to, but Expect, Relapse

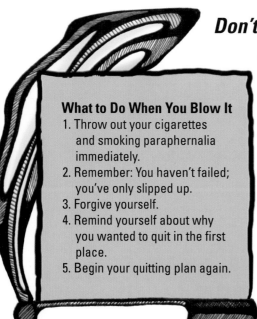

What to Do When You Blow It
1. Throw out your cigarettes and smoking paraphernalia immediately.
2. Remember: You haven't failed; you've only slipped up.
3. Forgive yourself.
4. Remind yourself about why you wanted to quit in the first place.
5. Begin your quitting plan again.

There is no easy way to break the nicotine habit. The U.S. Department of Health and Human Services estimates that within six months of quitting, nearly 80 percent of people who attempt to quit start smoking again. The American Lung Association estimates that the average successful quitter relapses two to four times before actually succeeding.

Millions of people who try to quit don't succeed the first time. But millions do eventually quit for good. How do they do it? They start again and again and again, after every relapse, until they finally reach their goal of being tobacco-free.

Relapse is a normal part of the quitting experience. Expect it, and don't let it convince you that it's impossible to be nicotine free once you've started using tobacco products. Recognize relapse for what it is—a temporary setback—and develop strategies to help you kick the habit for good.

CHAPTER

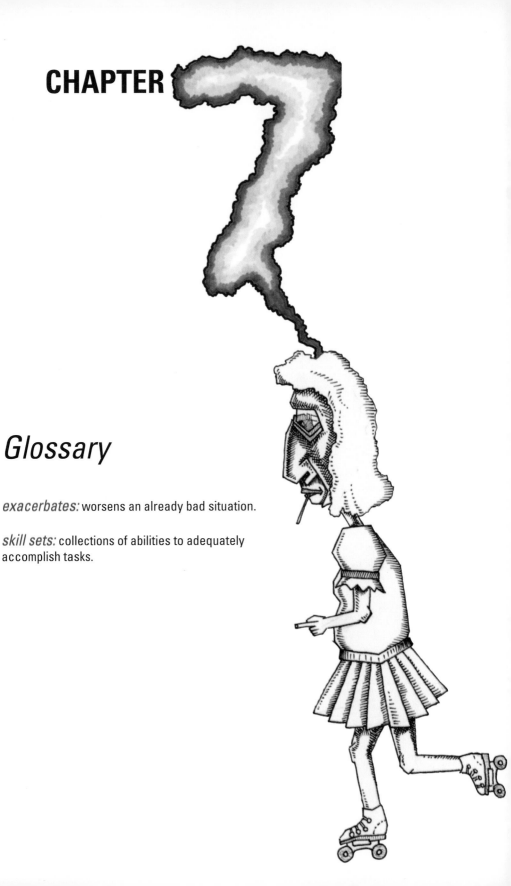

Glossary

exacerbates: worsens an already bad situation.

skill sets: collections of abilities to adequately accomplish tasks.

Smoke-Free for Life: Tips for Tossing Tobacco for Good

"I think the key [to successful quitting] is focusing on the positive. Build up the good things in your life, and the smoking will go away by itself. The thing I did that helped me the most was to set up one really fun thing to do every single day."

"My best advice for new quitters is to let it all out in whatever form seems most comfortable. If you're feeling lonely and scared, call up a friend. Ask for a hug. Talk it out, write it out, draw a picture or write a song about it, but you've got to let yourself feel it all—the joy and the pain both—without denying anything."

Giving up cigarettes doesn't just save you money; it is also a smart investment in your health and well-being.

"Don't feel sorry for yourself; be proud that you're standing up to your addiction."

"[Smoking] IS NOT WORTH IT. Though I am just nineteen, in the last year I have really grown to realize the importance of my body. I may still be young but my body WILL age with me and it will age more quickly if I don't take care of it. Our bodies are amazing tools, they are a gift and we should treat them that way."

"[Smoking] is an expensive habit that isn't really necessary. If I could go back, knowing what I know today about how it makes me feel and how much money I have spent on it, I probably would not have started smoking; there are better things to do with your time and money."

These words from former smokers illustrate how quitting smoking—the reasons for doing it, the methods used, the motivations behind the decision—vary with each person. Ultimately, only you know what will work for you. But something will work. You will be able to quit. The goal then is to stay

The Savings Add Up

If you smoked one $5 pack of cigarettes per day, here's how the money you save by quitting piles up:

After one day: $5
After one week: $35
After one month (30 days): $150
After two months (60 days): $300
After three months (90 days): $450
After six months (180 days): $900
After one year (52 weeks): $1,820
After five years: $9,100
After ten years: $18,200

Just by quitting smoking, in ten years you can save enough money to buy a new car.

nicotine-free. To do that, you'll need to develop specific coping skills for handling those emotions, actions, and situations you used to rely on nicotine to help you get through. For example, if you used to have a cigarette to help you handle a stressful situation, find something else that works. The National Cancer Institute identifies two categories of these coping skills:

1. Behavioral coping skills: the things you do or the actions you take to help you get through a situation and reduce your urge to smoke.
2. Mental coping skills: the things you think or tell yourself to help you manage and to reduce your urge to smoke.

Because the act of quitting and actions required to remain tobacco-free are much the same, these coping *skill sets* use many of the same strategies you learned in chapter 4 to help you overcome nicotine's psychological addiction. Here's a partial list of these coping skills:

Behavioral Coping Skills
Get rid of existing smoke odors.
Exercise.
Avoid circumstances and situations you associate with smoking.
Stay away from what tempts you.
Start a hobby that occupies your hands.
Keep your mouth busy (use sugar-free gum, lollipops, sugarless candy, or snack on crunchy or chewy foods).
Drink lots of water.
Start new habits and routines.

Exercise provides tangible rewards that reinforce your decision to become a nonsmoker.

Surround yourself with people who support and respect your choice to live a
healthier nonsmoking lifestyle.

Mental Coping Skills

Reward yourself.

Surround yourself with supportive friends.

Replace negative thinking with positive thinking.

Remember why you quit in the first place.

Treat each day as a brand new beginning.

Don't overlook these mental skills. So much of nicotine recovery depends on attitude. And the best way to improve your attitude about quitting is not to think of quitting as loss or self-denial. Those who relapse while trying to quit most often lose the battle of the mind. They think they've lost something good; they've given up something they enjoyed; they feel deprived. So they indulge in "just one more."

Rather than focusing on loss, think about gain. Concentrate on what you're gaining by quitting smoking: freedom to control your choices, better health, more spending money, a new network of friends, a chance at a better quality of life, freedom to become the best "you" you can be. Successful quitters "stay quit" by looking at what quitting gives them, not what it takes from them.

One of the biggest gains from giving up nicotine is better overall health. Doctors and researchers agree: Quitting

Did you know . . .
within 20 minutes of your last cigarette your body begins to heal?
within the first hour, as poisons leave your system, the oxygen in your blood rises to a normal level?
within an hour, your pulse rate returns to normal?
And within a few days . . .
    you'll taste and smell things better.
    you'll be able to breathe more easily.
    your cough will begin to improve.

smoking is *the* most important thing you can do for your health. More than 45 million Americans have given up the tobacco habit for good. So can you.

You Can Do It!

Imagine that you went to the doctor today, and he told you he had good news and bad news. What's the bad news? You have a 100 percent fatal disease that will start killing you immediately, but it will do so slowly and with much pain. You will die of this disease, and it will be an ugly death.

What's the good news? There is a cure, and your doctor holds it in his hand. All you have to do is take it to make it work.

What would you do? Would you ignore the cure and choose to die? Or would you make the choice to set yourself free from this terrifying disease and its ultimate outcome.

Of course, you'd grab the cure in an instant and begin your treatment right away.

Smoking causes or *exacerbates* many of America's leading health conditions today. Unlike some health problems, most of these can be stopped in their tracks by giving up smoking. It sounds like an easy solution, but as anyone who has tried to quit can tell you, it can be an extremely hard battle. Yet it's a battle worth fighting.

Further Reading

Bellenir, Karen, ed. *Tobacco Information for Teens: Health Tips about the Hazards of Using Cigarettes, Smokeless Tobacco, and Other Nicotine Products*. Detroit: Omnigraphics, 2007.

Brizer, David. *Quitting Smoking for Dummies*. Indianapolis: Wiley and Sons, 2003.

Esherick, Joan. *Clearing the Haze: A Teen's Guide to Smoking-Related Health Issues*. Broomall, Pa.: Mason Crest, 2005.

Hyde, Margaret O., and John F. Setaro. *Smoking 101: An Overview for Teens*. New York: Twenty-First Century Books, 2005.

Kleinman, Lowell, and Deborah Kleinman. *The Complete Idiot's Guide to Quitting Smoking*. Indianapolis: Alpha, 2000.

Miller, Barbara. *How to Quit Smoking Even if You Don't Want To*. Victoria, B.C., Canada: Trafford, 2001.

Wagner, Heather Lehr. *Nicotine*. New York: Chelsea House, 2003.

For More Information

American Cancer Society
www.cancer.org

American Heart Association
www.americanheart.org

American Heart Association's Smoking-Cessation page
www.americanheart.org/presenter.
jhtml?identifier=4731

American Lung Association
www.lungusa.org

Campaign for Tobacco-Free Kids
www.tobaccofreekids.org

Centers for Disease Control and Prevention (CDC)
www.cdc.gov

CDC's Nicotine and Tobacco Web Site
www.cdc.gov/tobacco

CDC's Quit Smoking page
www.cdc.gov/tobacco/quit_smoking

National Cancer Institute (NCI)
www.cancer.gov

NCI's Smoke-Free Web Site
www.smokefree.gov

National Institute on Drug Abuse (NIDA)
www.nida.nih.gov

National Institutes of Health (NIH)
www.nih.gov

National Library of Medicine's Smoking Information
page
www.nlm.nih.gov/medlineplus/smoking.html

NicNet
www.nicnet.org

Society for Research on Nicotine and Tobacco
www.srnt.org

Surgeon General's Tobacco Cessation Web site: You
Can Quit Smoking Now!
www.surgeongeneral.gov/tobacco

U.S. Department of Health and Human Services'
Nicotine Information Web Site
www.smokefree.org

U.S. Department of Health and Human Services'
National Quitline Number
1-800-QUITNOW

Publisher's note:
The Web sites listed on this page were active at the time of publication. The
publisher is not responsible for Web sites that have changed their addresses or
discontinued operation since the date of publication. The publisher will review
and update the Web-site list upon each reprint.

Bibliography

American Cancer Society. *Guide to Quitting Smoking.* http://www.cancer.org/docroot/PED/content/PED_10_13X_Guide_for_Quitting_Smoking.asp.

Campaign for Tobacco-Free Kids. *Smoking and Decreased Physical Performance.* Washington, D.C.: National Center for Tobacco-Free Kids, 2002.

———. *Toll of Tobacco in the United States of America.* Washington, D.C.: Campaign for Tobacco-Free Kids, 2007.

Carr, Allen. *The Little Book of Quitting.* New York: Sterling Publishing, 2005.

Ferguson, Tom. *The No-Nag, No-Guilt, Do-It-Your-Own-Way Guide to Quitting Smoking.* New York: Ballantine, 1987.

Forever Free: Life without Cigarettes. Gainesville: University of South Florida, H. Lee Moffit Cancer Center and Research Institute, Tobacco Research and Intervention Program, 2000.

Hirschfelder, Arlene. *Kick Butts! A Kid's Action Guide to a Tobacco-free America.* Parsippany, N.J.: Julian Messner, 1998.

Meeker-O'Connell, Ann. *How Nicotine Works.* http://health.howstuffworks.com/nicotine.htm.

National Cancer Institute. *Clearing the Air: Quit Smoking Today.* Bethesda, Md.: U.S. Department of Health and Human Services, National Institutes of Health, 2003. NIH Publication No. 03-1647.

———. *You Can Quit Smoking*. Bethesda, Md.: U.S. Department of Health and Human Services, National Institutes of Health, 2003.

———. *You Can Quit Smoking: 5-Day Countdown*. Bethesda, Md.: U.S. Department of Health and Human Services, National Institutes of Health, 2003.

———. *Fact Sheet: Handling Irritability and Frustration . . . Without Smoking*. Bethesda, Md.: U.S. Department of Health and Human Services, National Institutes of Health, 2004.

———. *Fact Sheet: Quitting Tobacco: Handling Stress . . . Without Smoking*. Bethesda, Md.: U.S. Department of Health and Human Services, National Institutes of Health, 2004.

———. *Fact Sheet: Quitting Tobacco: Short-Term and Long-Term Health Benefits*. Bethesda, Md.: U.S. Department of Health and Human Services, National Institutes of Health, 2004.

———. *The Truth about "Light" Cigarettes: Questions and Answers*. Bethesda, Md.: U.S. Department of Health and Human Services, National Institutes of Health, 2004.

National Institute on Drug Abuse. *Tobacco Addiction*. Bethesda, Md.: U.S. Department of Health and Human Services, National Institutes of Health, 2006. NIH Publication No. 06-4342.

National Institute on Drug Abuse for Teens. *The Science Behind Drug Abuse: Nicotine*. http://teens.drugabuse. gov/facts/facts_nicotine1.asp.

National Institutes of Health and the National Library of Medicine. *Nicotine*. http://www.nlm.nih.gov/medlineplus/ency/article/002510.htm.

———. *Nicotine Withdrawal*. http://www.nlm.nih.gov/medlineplus/ency/article/000953.htm.

———. *Smoking and Smokeless Tobacco*. http://www.nlm.nih.gov/medlineplus/ency/article/002032.htm.

———. *Smoking—Tips on How to Quit*. http://www.nlm.nih.gov/medlineplus/ency/article/001992.htm.

Pampel, Fred C. *Tobacco Industry and Smoking*. New York: Facts on File, Inc., 2004.

U.S. Department of Health and Human Services. *Frequently Asked Questions . . . About Quitting Smoking*. Atlanta: U.S. Department of Health and Human Services, Centers for Disease Control and Prevention, National Center for Chronic Disease Prevention and Health Promotion, Office on Smoking and Health, 2004.

———. *The Health Consequences of Smoking: What It Means to You*. Atlanta: U.S. Department of Health and Human Services, Centers for Disease Control and Prevention, National Center for Chronic Disease Prevention and Health Promotion, Office on Smoking and Health, 2004.

Wetherall, Charles F. Quit. Philadelphia: Running Press, 2001.

Index

addiction 35–40
acetaminophen 44
acupuncture 72–73
American Cancer Society,
    the 33, 52, 75, 83, 86, 104,
    106
*American Journal of
Preventative Medicine* 23

butts, cigarette 12,

cancer 13, 19, 84
Centers for Disease Control
    20, 24–25, 52, 104

D.A.R.E 13

further reading 103

Google 71
Green, Doctor Joseph 72

herbal remedies 74
Hypnosis 71–72

National Cancer Institute,
The 52, 98, 104, 106
    and its Four Step
        Program 79
    and the Five-Day
        Countdown 80
nicotine 12-13, 21, 24, 55
    and addiction 31-44

and behavior 55, 58–59,
    61, 65-66, 69
and hormones 35-38
and quitting 76–77,
    79–81, 85–93, 98, 101
and medical aids 44–53
and the nervous system
    34, 37–38
and nicotine poisoning 46
Nicotine Replacement
Therapy (NRT) 44-50
    and nicotine patches
        45–46
    and nicotine gum 46–47
    and nasal sprays 47–48
    and oral inhalers 48–49
    and lozenges 49–50

peer pressure 13, 27
prescription drugs
    Chantix 51–52
    Zyban 50–51, 53
programs for quitting
    Great American
        Smokeout 75–76

quitting
    and cravings 92
    and health benefits of 86
    and emotional benefits of
        26–27
    and emotional effects of
        91

and others 89–90
and relapsing 92–93
and rewards for 67
and personal strategies
      for 83–88
and stories of 55–56, 69
and stress 62–63
and the survival kit 66
and weight gain 58

smoking
      and addiction to, 31–41
      and alternatives to 63
      and deaths caused by 14
      and diseases caused by
            14,19
      and health risks caused
            by 25–26
      and monetary cost of,
            12, 14–17

and neo-natal effects of
      20
and physical effects of
      23–24
and pregnancy 21
and psychological effects
      of 38–40
and "Smoker's Face" 41
and stories of 11–13,
      17–23
and triggers of 59–61
Surgeon General of the
      United States 13, 25, 33,
            79, 105
      and the 1964 report on
            smoking 14
      and its Four Step Program
            77

Picture Credits

Centers for Disease Control and Prevention: pp. 12, 20, 51

Dreamstime.com
  Dimistudio: p. 92
  Hannamariah: p. 90

GNU Free Documentation license, Version 1.2
  RegBarc: p. 45

istockphoto.com: pp.22, 37
  Bergeron, Ian: p. 22
  Blaneyphoto: p. 96
  Patterson, Anita: p. 30

Jupiter Images: pp. 47,84, 87,89

LifeArt: pp. 48, 64

Medisphere
  Allen, Steve: p. 68

Morbidity and Mortality Weekly Report: p. 15

PhotoDisc: pp. 34, 57, 68, 75, 99

PhotoLink
  Pearce, S.: p. 20

Surveillance Epidemiology and End Results (SEER), a program of the National Cancer Institute (NCI): p. 18

Author/Consultant Biographies

Author

Though never a smoker, Joan Esherick watched loved ones battle with nicotine addictions for over three decades. She observed firsthand the toll chronic lung disease takes on the body and soul as she watched COPD slowly compromise her father's quality of life and lead to his death. The author of twenty-five nonfiction books, including *Clearing the Haze: A Teen's Guide to Smoking-Related Health Issues,* Joan lives in southeastern Pennsylvania with her husband, their three children, and four Labrador retrievers.

Consultant

Wade Berrettini, the consultant for *Smoking: The Dangerous Addiction*, received his MD from Jefferson Medical College and a PhD in Pharmacology from Thomas Jefferson University. For ten years, Dr. Berrettini served as a Fellow at the National Institutes of Health in Bethesda, Maryland, where he studied the genetics of behavioral disorders. Currently Dr. Berrettini is the Karl E. Rickels Professor of Psychiatry and Director, Center for Neurobiology and Behavior at the University of Pennsylvania in Philadelphia. He is also an attending physician at the Hospital of the University of Pennsylvania.

Dr. Berrettini is the author or co-author of more than 250 scientific articles as well as several books. He has conducted ground-breaking genetic research in nicotine addiction. He is the holder of two patents and the recipient of several awards, including recognition by Best Doctors in America 2003–2004, 2005–2006, and 2007–2008.